Rereading *Capital*

Rereading *Capital*

BEN FINE and
LAURENCE HARRIS

New York   Columbia University Press   1979

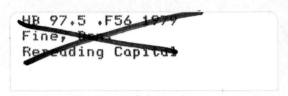
Printed in Great Britain

Library of Congress Cataloging in Publication Data

Fine, Ben.
   Rereading Capital.

   Bibliography: p.
   Includes index.
   1. Marxian economics.   2. Marx, Karl, 1818–1883.   Das
Kapital.   I. Harris, Laurence, joint author.   II. Title.
HB97.5.F56   1979   335.4'1   78–20912
ISBN 0–231–04792–4

Contents

Part II

Preface

This book concerns Marx's theory of the capitalist economy and, in particular, its applicability to the study of current economic events. Although the subjects about which we have written include many which appear to be highly abstract they are all ultimately relevant to the analysis of concrete events. Indeed, our collaboration on the study of value theory, laws of tendency and related concepts grew out of our collaboration on the analysis of the economic events which filled the newspapers every day; we found that if we were to go beyond Keynesian and other orthodox analyses it was necessary to consider the foundations of Marxist analysis. This study took place while both authors were engaged in the activities of the Conference of Socialist Economists, and since there already existed within the CSE a significant body of work concerned with the foundations of Marxist economics our work necessarily starts out with that as its raw material. Accordingly this book has a dual character as a critical survey of and a contribution to the continuing debate.

We consider that as a contribution to the development of Marxist economics this book is particularly important in emphasising that in order to analyse concrete events the theory of the capitalist mode of production must be developed through several levels of abstraction until it is ultimately able to grasp the complexities of the concrete. Marx's own theory of the capitalist mode in *Capital* and elsewhere is at the highest level of abstraction, but in our view it is the indispensable basis for the development of less abstract analyses. Two aspects of this development are particularly noted in this book; the first is the necessity to theorise the *periodisa-*

tion of capitalism into stages (for otherwise it is impossible to consider either the specific aspects of modern capitalism or the history of capitalist societies); the second is the necessity to theorise the existence of *national states,* for at *Capital*'s level of abstraction the national state is not a developed concept.

No book on Marxist theory can be easy to read, but we have made every effort to write in an accessible style. Our intention is that the book should be of interest to and comprehensible to anyone, whether economist or not, who has made a study of *Capital* and reached the level of understanding at which textbooks such as Ben Fine's *Marx's Capital* (Macmillan) or Paul Sweezy's *Theory of Capitalist Development* (Monthly Review Press) are aimed.

All material in this book is new rather than being reprints of material that has appeared elsewhere. Nevertheless, Chapters 2, 3 and 4 owe much to the fact that we were able to develop our ideas at an earlier stage and enter into a discussion of them by publishing them in the *Socialist Register 1976* and *1977.* We are therefore most grateful to the editors, Ralph Miliband and John Saville, for publishing and encouraging us to write 'Controversial Issues in Marxist Economic Theory' and 'Surveying the Foundations'.

We are very heavily indebted to Gillian Robinson for typing the manuscript with great speed and remarkably good cheer. Several colleagues have given us assistance and advice and we have also benefited from discussions with our students at Birkbeck. We thank them all for their help without listing them. We must, however, acknowledge with gratitude the fact that Judith Shapiro brought to our attention the point made in Chapter 3 about the Fundamentalists' erroneous interpretation of Marx on Smith. We also wish to thank the Warden and Fellows of Nuffield College, Oxford, for the facilities and hospitality given to Ben Fine in 1977 when he was on sabbatical leave and working on this book.

The Index was compiled by Wing Commander Roger F. Pemberton, M.C., T.D., to whom we extend our thanks.

February 1978   BEN FINE
                                              LAURENCE HARRIS

Part I

1
Method and the Structure of Capital

1.1 The Circuit of Capital

In this book we present and intervene in debates between Marxists concerning the study of the capitalist mode of production (CMP). This mode was the object of Marx's mature work (in particular of *Capital* and *Theories of Surplus Value*) and he brought to bear on it a specifically materialist method of study. We take Marx's work as our benchmark in appraising the debates. This does not mean that Marx's conclusions are incontrovertible, but that subsequent writings must be judged in the light of Marx's method. If a particular theory (such as the body known as neo-Ricardianism) produces a conclusion in opposition to Marx's, we ask first whether it does so by contravening Marx's method and, if it does, we attempt to judge whether there are any grounds for thinking that the alternative method is in some sense better.

Because of the significance we attach to Marx's method in our criterion we begin the book with this chapter setting out its principle features. Such a task is by its nature relatively dry. In an attempt to overcome this and to give content to the ideas involved – levels of abstraction, mode of production, relations of production etc. – we shall illustrate them in terms of the industrial circuit of capital. The remainder of this section describes this circuit which, precisely because capital is 'the all-dominating economic power of bourgeois society', is central to Marx's analysis of the CMP.

Capital is itself a social relation: specifically it is the social relation involved in the self-expansion of value, the produc-

3

tion, appropriation and accumulation of surplus value. Capital, being self-expanding value, is essentially a process, the process of reproducing value and producing new value. In other words, capital is value in the process of reproducing itself as capital and, being a process, it is in a state of motion. The circuit of capital describes this motion and it highlights the fact that capital takes different forms in its circuit or reproduction process. The social relation which is capital successively assumes and relinquishes as clothing the forms of money, productive capital and commodities.

If we begin with *money capital, M*, this is exchanged for commodities, *C*, part of which consist of physical means of production, *MP*, the value of which is constant capital, *C*, and part of which consist of labour-power, *LP*, whose value is variable capital, *V*. These elements of production are brought together through exchange – the method peculiar to the capitalist mode of production – and are set to work under capitalist relations of production and at this stage of the circuit capital has assumed the form of *productive capital*. The result of the production process is the creation of new commodities, *C'*, owned by the capitalist, and in taking this form capital becomes *commodity capital*. The value of these commodities is greater than that of the commodity inputs by the amount by which the labour performed in the production process exceeds the value of labour-power. Consequently, the commodities embody surplus value, so that, when they are sold for money (i.e. exchanged or realised), capital reassumes the money form, *M'*, but with quantity of money-capital greater than that with which the circuit began. This circuit can be represented as follows:

$$M - C \underset{MP}{\overset{LP}{<}} \dots P \dots C' - M' \text{ or in circular form}$$

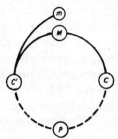

where *m* represents the difference between *M'* and *M*.

Marx divided this circuit into two spheres of activity. The activity of setting to work means of production and labour-power to produce new commodities; that is, the activity *C*(*MP, LP*) . . . *P* . . . *C'* on the circuit takes place in the *sphere of production*. The activity of selling the commodities for money and buying commodities as inputs, the activity *C'*−*M'*−*C* (*MP, LP*) takes place in the *sphere of exchange*. Although the two spheres are distinguished the circuit of capital implies the necessity of their unity, so that capital can only be understood in terms of the circuit as a whole. While, at the moment, the specific features of this unity appear to be a simple division of activity between the production and the realisation of surplus value, the unity of the two spheres is complex in the process of economic reproduction as a whole.

So far we have only considered the industrial circuit of an *individual* capitalist. But this presupposes the existence of other individual circuits, with which capital in the forms of money and commodities is exchanged; and it presupposes the reproduction of labour-power as a commodity (i.e. the reproduction of the class relations of production), etc. In this light, an understanding of the spheres of production and exchange is insufficient for understanding the structure of the capitalist economy. In addition, Marx introduces the concept of *distribution*. The distribution of values between (and within) classes in the capitalist mode of production is a process which encompasses both the spheres of production and exchange and it can only be understood in terms of its complex unity with production and exchange.

Marx states this in the *Grundrisse*. His conclusion is 'not that production, distribution, exchange and consumption are identical, but that they all form the members of a totality, distinctions within a unity. Production predominates not only over itself . . . but over the other moments as well . . . A definite production thus determines a definite consumption, distribution and exchange as well *as definite relations between these different moments*. Admittedly, however, – production is itself determined by the other moments. . . . Mutal interaction takes place between the different moments.' Thus, to use language currently in vogue, production, exchange and distribution are to be seen as members of a structured whole, a totality in which production is determinant but the other spheres have a relative autonomy and each sphere has an effect on each other. This poses the task of exploring the relationships between the spheres of economic activity. It is a fault common to many of the modern Marxist economists, that they are unable to grasp this complex structure as a whole and analyse it with a bias of one sort or another emphasising one or more of the spheres at the expense of others. Such biases cannot be corrected simply by appending the missing elements, for these will have been consistently absent from the outset and can only be restored by a reconstruction of the analysis in its entirety.

1.2   Method of Abstraction

We are now in a position to consider what, for Marx, comprises the method of science and to illustrate it in terms of the circuit of capital. It is well known that Marx described science as a process of producing knowledge by going behind the superficial appearance of things: 'But all science would be superfluous if the outward appearance and essence of things directly coincided.' But going behind superficial appearances is no simple task. First, the phenomena which lie behind the appearances (or the concepts of these phenomena) are not simply there waiting to be found. Starting from experience of the complex world of appearances and from existing scientific and ideological attempts to understand this experience, science has the task of producing the concepts appropriate to these hidden phenomena. And, second, science does not simply remain at the stage of conceptualising the hidden essential phenomena; its task is to produce knowledge of how they determine and give rise to the phenomena which are apparent, observable and conceptualised in everyday experience.

These tasks of science are fulfilled in Marx's method. In the *Grundrisse* he describes it as starting from the complexity of the superficial world and constructing the most simple, highly abstract concepts. From these, with their interrelations and their internal contradictions, increasingly complex concepts are developed until the complexity of the world of appearances is reproduced in thought or on the page. The important point is that this process is neither purely idealist, existing in thought independent of reality, nor arbitrary. Instead, the concepts produced and their logical order are in accordance with material reality. The process of abstraction can be illustrated in terms of the circuit of capital. The concepts of the commodity and of money are relatively simple and at a high level of abstraction (although not at the same level since money is predicated upon the existence of commodities), but by developing these concepts and their connections with the production and expansion of value the concept of capital is produced. Thus capital and its forms such as money-capital and commodity-capital are more complex concepts than money and commodities as such. And this is true not only at the level of ideas but also in reality. In reality the social relations involved in capital are not necessary preconditions for commodity exchange and money, but these on the other hand *are* necessary preconditions for capitalist social relations.

Another example, a particularly important one, of Marx's method of abstraction is the division of the circuit of capital into spheres. The essential thing about the circuit of capital is the unity of the spheres of production and exchange: the production *and* realisation of surplus value are essential functions of capital, and production and exchange both affect each other. But Marx constructs the concept of the circuit as a whole by producing the theory of capitalist production while abstracting from exchange, and the theory of commodity exchange while abstracting from production.

The last example of the process of abstraction which we will consider is the fact that the circuit of industrial capital is, itself, a simple concept. The idea of it is developed by abstracting from the existence of competition. It is the circuit of social capital as a whole considered as capital-in-general. It can be conceived as that of an individual capital if the latter is considered as simply a 'representative' part of capital-in-general. But the circuit of an individual capital in fact presupposes the existence of other individual circuits with which competitive exchange takes place. The circuit of capital is a concept developed by abstracting from this competition. For this reason it can be treated in terms of capital-in-general. But, having developed the concept, Marx transforms it by then producing the concept of competition between capitals and integrating it with that of social capital. Again, this thought process parallels those of reality; in reality competition between capitals is predicated upon the circuit of capital-in-general (and the circuits of individual capitals in so far as these are independent of competition) for without the relations *between capital and labour* encompassed by those simple circuits competition *between capitals* cannot exist. Related to this is the fact that the spheres of production and exchange are, even when integrated, relatively simple concepts which exist in abstraction from distribution. On the basis of these spheres (and with competition between capital and labour, and between capitals) distribution of values between and within classes is analysed.

1.3   Determination by Production

In Marx's economic analysis his propositions are dominated by a major idea, that the sphere of production is fundamental to the economy as a whole:

> not that production, distribution, exchange and consumption are identical, but that they all form the members of a totality, distinctions within a unity. Production predominates not only over itself . . . but over the other moments as well. . . . A definite production determines a definite consumption, distribution and exchange as well as definite relations between these different moments.

This is an extremely controversial idea; its validity is denied implicitly in many economic theories and is explicitly questioned by, for example, Hodgson (1977). To understand it is fundamental to an understanding of Marx's method of abstraction. For the very concept of *production as such*, as a moment of the circuit of capital, can only be understood as production in abstraction from exchange and distribution (for production articulated with these other spheres is the whole circuit rather than one of its moments).

In order to understand the simple concept of the sphere of production it must be understood that 'abstracting from exchange and distribution' is not the same as 'ignoring exchange and distribution', nor as assuming that they do not exist. On the contrary, the precondition for *capitalist* production is that commodities are produced for exchange and that distribution is based upon wage labour. But in conceptualising capitalist production as such Marx is concerned with the production process in circumstances where only the most elementary type of exchange (exchange between workers and capitalists) exists and where this exchange proceeds smoothly (without, for example, realisation crises). Similarly, only the most elementary distribution relations (wages equal to the value of labour-power) are assumed to exist in the analysis of production.

With the concept of the sphere of production clarified, it becomes necessary to clarify the meaning of determination by the sphere of production. Marx makes clear that there is not a simple one way causal relationship from production to exchange and distribution: 'Admittedly, however, . . . production is itself determined by the other moments.' Each sphere affects the other, but production in a basic sense determines the whole economic process. But what is meant by 'in a basic sense determines' or 'ultimately predominates'? A weak interpretation is that without production there can be no exchange or distribution, but such a statement is hardly controversial. A stronger interpretation is that on the basis of particular relations of production arise particular modes of exchange and distribution.

This interpretation is the basis of our defence of value analysis (Fine and Harris (1977)) and we return to it below (Chapter 2). The point is that because the abstraction called the sphere of production explicitly considers exchange only in the simple form of worker/capitalist intercourse, it deals with the struggle of the two great classes uncomplicated by struggle between capitalists themselves (which would have to be introduced if we were to consider full competitive exchange) or the struggles of other classes, fractions, or strata. And this antagonistic relation between capital and labour, at the centre of the sphere of production, is what differentiates the capitalist from other modes of production. On the basis of these particularly capitalist relations of production, and hence on the basis of the production of surplus value, arise specifically capitalist relations of exchange and distribution. Equalisation of the rate of profit, for example, is a distributional law which for Marx has no meaning unless surplus value is produced (in the sphere of production) and transformed into profit (in the sphere of exchange). In this example it is clearly seen that the existence of specifically capitalist exchange and distribution relations is based on the capitalist relations of production which, in the antagonism between labour and capital, ensure the production of surplus value. The example, however, begs a question: why argue that the surplus which is produced takes the form of surplus value rather than directly taking the form of profit so that exchange and distribution are not treated as dependent on production but conterminous with it? We consider that question, as posed by Hodgson (1977), below (Chapter 2).

To say that specifically capitalist forms of exchange and distribution are based on the existence of capitalist relations of production is, however, not as strong as saying that the history of these spheres is determined by the history of production. But this strong statement, that the ups and downs and convolutions of the economy are determined by production even though they may manifest themselves in the spheres of exchange (a change in effective demand) or distribution (a change in the rate of profit), is what Marx is saying when he refers to determination by production. The quotation above (p. 5) indicates that exchange and distribution have in Marx's view an effect on production: a decline in effective demand resulting from the collapse of the credit system and originating, therefore, in the sphere of exchange can cause a crisis in production, as could a decline in industrial capital's profit rate which for some arbitrary reason originates in the sphere of distribution. But Marx's proposition is that such occurrences are not basic to capitalist laws of development; instead, conditions in the sphere of production determine developments and even if a crisis, for example, first manifests itself in a decline in demand or a decline in profit this is generally a consequence of developments in the *production* of value and surplus value. Again, this is something that can only be understood on the basis of Marx's method of abstraction, for it is only by separating developments in exchange and distribution from those in production that the dependence of the former on the latter can be theorised and understood. We shall return to this later in the context of the law of the tendency of the rate of profit to fall (Chapter 4).

There are then, two hierarchical structures. One is the hierarchy of concepts produced in thought in the movement from the simple to the complex, from high to low levels of abstraction. The other is the hierarchy of reality, the real relationships of determination between real phenomena. The two hierarchies do not directly correspond in any simple manner but there is a definite and necessary relation between them. The absence of a simple correspondence is illustrated by the fact that although in reality the behaviour of commodity exchange and money is determined by capital accumulation, in the hierarchy of concepts Marx has to analyse first commodities and money (and then transform the concepts on the basis of the concept of capital). The existence of a necessary relation between the two hierarchies is given from the fact that the hierarchy of levels of abstraction of concepts is not arbitrary. As well as being a theory of reality it is simultaneously a product of that theory and therefore has a definite relation to the reality which is being analysed. This does not provide a guarantee of the 'truth' of the theory, but at the same time it precludes the relativist idea that any hierarchy of concepts is as good as any other. The hierarchy of determination in reality is conceived as one where production is determinant, but for Marx this is not only the conclusion of the analysis but also its starting-point (that is, the relation of concepts is not only the theory but also the product of the theory). As Marx makes clear at the beginning of his famous statement of the materialist conception of history (in the *Preface to a Contribution to a Critique of Political Economy*) determination by production is: 'The general conclusion at which I arrived and . . . once reached, continued to serve as the leading thread in my studies.' This principle of determination by production is treated as a general principle of history, but the exact manner of its operation is specific for each mode of production. Each mode has a specific structure of relations between production, distribution and exchange. Moreover exactly what comprises each of these moments of economic reproduction cannot be defined as general concepts but only as specific to particular modes. As one example exchange consists of market relations in some modes but not others. As another, sexual reproduction can comprise production in a slave mode but not under capitalism. It is worth noting that this specificity of the concepts and real categories precludes the possibility of a general theory of modes of production such as that which Balibar, in Althusser and Balibar (1970), attempts. For him one mode differs from another simply in terms of the way that universal categories (labourer, non-labourer and means of production) are combined, but this ignores the specificity to each mode of the categories of phenomena which exist within it.

1.4 Mode of Production and Social Formation

When we say, as we do at the beginning of this chapter, that the debates we are surveying concern the capitalist mode of production we raise the question of what is meant by the CMP or by a mode of production whether capitalist or not. This problem is an aspect of the method of abstraction.

Marx uses the concept of mode of production in several senses, sometimes referring specifically to production, sometimes to the economic process as a whole, and sometimes to all social relations which include political and ideological as well as economic relations. Following Althusser and Balibar (1970) and Poulantzas (1973) we adopt the last, all-embracing, concept of a mode of production. But however narrow or all-embracing the concept, the important thing is that Marx produced it as a highly abstract concept. The society in which we live is not itself a mode of production nor is it reproduced in all its complexity in the concept of the mode of production. Instead, the concept of the society in which we actually live is that of a particular *social formation* such as 'Britain in 1978' while the CMP is a concept which is more general and more abstract.

The CMP is defined by forces of production (techniques) and relations of production and an articulation between the two all of which are specific to capital. The articulation between forces and relations is such that the relations of production are determinant. In particular, in the CMP in a mature stage of development the forces of production are characterised by machine production and, corresponding to this, the relations by the real subordination of labour to capital (on which see Brighton Labour Process Group (1977) and *Capital*, vol. I, appendix (1976)). The relations of production in the CMP are characterised by the distribution and control of means of production such that the owners of the means of production and of the product of labour are the non-workers while workers own only the commodity labour-power. On the basis of these concepts the CMP is theorised by Marx and knowledge of its laws of development is produced. But the CMP is not the same as the British social formation (or world or any other social formation) and its laws of development are not the same as British history. Two facts are sufficient to make this clear. First, the CMP is a theory of the relations between two classes, the bourgeoisie and proletariat (the supports of capital and labour), whereas social formations have within them other classes as well; the petty-bourgeoisie and peasantry for example. Second, the history of a social formation unfolds over a definite scale of chronological time and with a definite sequence which varies from one capitalist social formation to another, whereas the laws of development of the CMP are not related to any time scale and are universal. It should, however, be noted that the concept of a mode of production is a subject of debate. The most systematic criticism of the concept has come from Hindess and Hirst (1977) and Cutler, Hindess, Hirst and Hussain (1977) (1978). We shall not enter into that debate here, but see Harris (1978).

If the idea of a social formation is more complex than the simple, highly abstract idea of a mode of production we have to specify the relationship between the two. Althusser (1969) and Althusser and Balibar (1970) argue that any particular social formation is the articulation of different modes of production. Twentieth-century France, for example, is a formation in which the CMP is dominant but there are also other modes of production comprised within this social formation as witnessed by the existence of the peasantry, a class which has no role in the CMP itself. A social formation, therefore, is in this conception a whole social entity which is the product of several modes of production, more fundamental social wholes, articulated with each other. A capitalist social formation is one which is the product of the CMP dominating the other constituent modes. It should be emphasised that in thinking of social formations as being produced by the articulation of different modes of production we do not mean that they are simply different modes stacked on to each other. Instead, as Poulantzas (1975) argues, social formations are the conditions of existence of their constituent modes of production. It should also be noted that although it is common to identify a social formation with a 'nation' or national state this is incorrect. A social formation may be a set of national social formations (even the world) or may be smaller than a national state.

In this book we concentrate on the analysis of the capitalist *mode of production* rather than particular social formations. It will be seen, however (Chapters 7, 8, 9), that this does not restrict analysis to a static, formalistic type of concept where nothing can be said about variations in the forms which exist; the fractionalisation of classes, the development of credit structures, the forms of state and so on. On the contrary, the periodisation of the capitalist mode of production forces and enables Marxists to understand these.

Although we distinguish between modes of production and social formations, one being a concept at a higher level of abstraction than the other, we consider that it is wrong to consider either as a uniquely defined concept of a social whole. That is, it is wrong to counterpose to each other just two levels of abstraction, one pertaining to the mode and the other to the social formation, as do Althusser and Poulantzas. Instead of being forced by jumping from one very high level of abstraction to one low level, the concept of concrete social formations is to be produced by proceeding from the most highly abstract to a *succession* of less abstract concepts until the concept of concrete social formations is produced. For example, the most abstract concept of the capitalist mode of production abstracts from the existence of nations and national states, but to produce on the basis of it the concept of the nation and national state still leaves us with a relatively abstract concept of the social whole; it remains a concept of the mode of production and is only one small step further toward the concept of the concrete social formation (Britain in the 1970s for example).

1.5   The Structure of *Capital*

No understanding of Marx's economics and no appraisal of modern Marxist writing is possible without an understanding of *Capital*. For this purpose it is essential to conclude this chapter by presenting the structure of the book and showing how it is related both to Marx's method of abstraction and to the hierarchical structure of the capitalist economy. For the structure of the book is neither arbitrary nor simple; it is an articulation of two structures, one of abstraction determined by the necessity of constructing increasingly complex concepts from the most abstract ones, the other of determination dictated by what in Marx's theory are the fundamental and what the dependent spheres of the economy. The structure which depends on the hierarchical nature of the economy is indicated in the titles of the volumes. Volume I, *Capitalist Production*, is concerned with the processes in the sphere of production. Volume II, *The Process of Circulation of Capital* analyses the sphere of exchange in its relation to production. It is therefore concerned with the circulation of capital between the two spheres. Because production is the determinant sphere, it is necessary that it be analysed before the interrelation of exchange and production is reached in volume II. Volume III, *Capitalist Production as a Whole*, is concerned with the distribution that has its basis in the integrated spheres of production and exchange. Although this structure is indicated in the titles of the three volumes, the actual structure of *Capital* corresponding to the structure of the economy is somewhat less schematic. The first point is that even in volume I exchange is present, but it is only present to the extent that is necessary for the existence of specifically capitalist production. That is, exchange of commodities between the capitalist class as a whole (the agents of capital-in-general) and the whole working class (agents of labour) is introduced in volume I in considering the process of production. Exchange between capitalists (capitals) themselves is not introduced until volume II (the reproduction schema) and then more fully developed in volume III. The second point is that distribution relations are present in volumes I and II, but only to the limited extent that they can be developed without the full development of exchange relations (inter-capitalist exchange) in volume III. For example, in volume I we have a discussion of the cyclical changes in the value of wages but this, far from being a full theory of distribution, is all that can be done when only the exchanges between the working class and bourgeoisie are present. This procedure for studying exchange and distribution incompletely at first and subsequently in developed form accords with Marx's view of the real structure of the economy; inter-capitalist exchange and the distribution of profit, interest, etc., between capitalists is in reality dependent upon the sphere of production and the exchanges between capital as a whole and labour.

The structure which is based on Marx's method of abstraction and the process of producing successively more complex concepts is related to but distinct from the structure just considered. For example, the concept of capital itself is successively re-produced and transformed in *Capital* until the unity of its three articulated spheres, production, exchange and distribution is produced as a complex concept. Moreover, even though capital is 'the all-dominating economic power of bourgeois society' even the most simple abstract concept of it is not the proper starting place for Marx. Capital is not introduced until Chapter 4. He starts with the much simpler abstract categories of the commodity and (derived from it) money – thereby introducing the general concept of exchange before production – and from these he produces the concept of capital. A second example of the increasing complexity of concepts is the development and presentation of increasingly complex concepts of inter-capitalist competition. Marx, in fact, introduces a concept of competition in volume I although that volume is essentially concerned with capital-in-general, rather than many-capitals in competition. There we find the analysis of competition between different capitals within one industry for this can be considered without the idea of exchange between capitalists. The fully developed idea of competition between industrial capitals is, however, not introduced until volume III, and there the concept is transformed into that of competition between capitals in different industries so as to equalise the rate of profit and form the general profit rate. Finally, on the basis of the concept of the general rate of profit, those of interest, merchant's profit and rent are developed by analysing the most complex form of competition, that which embraces competition between different fractions of the bourgeoisie (industrial, merchant and financial capitalists) and also the landlord class. A third and most important example of the increasing complexity of concepts as *Capital* unfolds, is the concept of value. At first in volumes I and II it is treated by abstracting from the quantitative divergence between value and exchange value but in volume III it is transformed into the concept of price of production (modified value) which is a qualitatively distinct and quantitatively different form of value. It is qualitatively distinct in that it is more complex. The significance of this particular concept, and the errors of one common interpretation of value that occur precisely because it fails to comprehend the process of abstraction, are explained below (Chapter 2).

Quite apart from the structure of *Capital* there remains the question of its *object*. It is the theory of the economic level in the capitalist mode of production. But that statement requires elaboration. By mode of production we mean, as explained above, a social whole constituting distinct but unified political, ideological and economic levels. Most important, we mean a highly abstract concept. Therefore Marx is not presenting the theory of a particular society, Britain or Europe in the mid-nineteenth century, but of the general laws which underlie and determine the economic process in all capitalist social formations (even though the forms in which the effects of these laws make their appearance differ from one social formation to another and, as we explain below (Chapters 7, 8, 9), from one stage of capitalism to another). The fact that *Capital* is concerned with this highly abstract concept is not invalidated by the inclusion in it of data and historical studies relating to the concrete phenomena of Britain and other social formations, for these serve the function of illustration alone. That Marx is not dealing with the whole of the CMP, but only with its economic level is important. It means that *Capital* does not contain the theory of politics nor of ideology. Nevertheless, there is discussion of the capitalist state in the passages on the Factory Acts and Marx does theorise the role of the state in the process of capitalism's birth. This, however, is not evidence of a theory of politics (for the state is not itself politics and is, in any case, not fully considered). And there is extensive discussion of ideology throughout *Capital* (especially the discussion of commodity fetishism) and in *Theories of Surplus Value*. But this is not present as a general theory of ideology in the capitalist mode; it concerns only ideological conceptions of the economy. Its function instead is to locate Marx's science of the economy with respect to the 'raw materials' which Marx appropriated at the outset and transformed in his critique of political economy.

1.6 Poles of Controversy

In relation to the structure of *Capital* and its concept of the capitalist economy it is now possible to survey the debates of Marxist political economy in a critical fashion. For the contributions to the debates are themselves orientated towards an interpretation of these structures. In the case of the structure of *Capital*, this is often direct and explicit with attempts at on the one hand affirmation and regurgitation or on the other criticism and reconstruction of Marx's analysis. In interpreting the structure of the capitalist economy, however, the contributions have been less conscious of the implications of their analyses, but these are, nevertheless, clearly defined. The protagonists in the debates can be classified into two schools of thought, neo-Ricardian and Fundamentalist (sometimes called capital-logicians), with some writers falling in between.

For neo-Ricardians all analysis of the capitalist economy takes place in the spheres of exchange and distribution. Since both are only examined in isolation from the sphere of production the result is the antithesis of Marx's analysis, for the latter emphasises the dependence of exchange and distribution on production and the impossibility of understanding capital except in the complex unity of the three spheres. Some neo-Ricardian writings do consider such things as changes in technique which should fall within the sphere of production. But even here the determinants are taken to be wage rates and profits which are exchange-based distributional categories. Moreover, and related to this one-sidedness, neo-Ricardians develop their conclusions only in terms of categories such as prices of production and market prices which exist at a relatively low level of abstraction. The ultimate theoretical justification for this approach is found in neo-Ricardianism's treatment of the transformation problem which Marx attempted (and failed adequately) to solve in volume III of *Capital*. Neo-Ricardians see the problem as one of deriving commodities' prices of production from the labour embodied in them and, concluding that prices of production can be quantified directly without quantifying values, they consider value theory to be an irrelevant diversion. Concomitantly, analysis of the sphere of production in abstraction, for which value theory is necessary, is rejected. From this follows a rejection by neo-Ricardians of Marx's distinction between productive and unproductive labour, for the distinction between these categories is central to Marx's concept of the fundamental determining role of the sphere of production and it is only relevant within a view which takes as central the relations between the *three* spheres. There follows their conclusion that economic crises are to be explained solely in terms of class struggle over distribution in the sphere of exchange (but there is also an implicit denial of the concept of economic class struggle and economic crises as such and an identification of economic activity with political activity).

For Fundamentalists, the sphere of production is determinant. Indeed, it is the only sphere of economic activity that they analyse in a consistent manner. In doing so the Fundamentalists emphasize the significance of value theory, assert that the conclusions drawn by neo-Ricardianism from the transformation problem are invalid, consider important the distinction between productive and unproductive labour and locate the source of crises in the tendency of the rate of profit to fall. The source of this tendency is itself located in the nature of capital-in-general and it is treated as the development of capital's contradictions with the fundamental contradiction located in the sphere of production.

An understanding of the positions taken by these two schools and by the several writers who are identified neither with one nor the other, can only be gained by examining the specific issues over which debates have taken place. We make a heuristic division between the issues. In Chapters 2 and 3 we examine the essentially 'static' issues of the transformation problem and the productive/unproductive labour distinction. These bring to the fore the differences over the significance of the concept of value, over the relationship between values and prices of production, and over the relationship between production, exchange and circulation. In Chapters 4 and 5 we show how these differences are reflected in differences over 'dynamic' issues, the economic laws of motion of capitalism. We examine the disputes over the law of the tendency of the rate of profit to fall and over the concept of crises. In Part I we examine capitalist economic reproduction in abstraction from social reproduction in general (i.e. political and ideological relations). This poses the problem of the relationship between economic and social reproduction, itself a controversial issue of Marxist political economy that has been debated in the context of the role of the state in capitalist society. We consider these issues in Part II, subsequently locating the analysis in terms of the reproduction of the world economy and contributions to an understanding of imperialism.

2
Value, Price and the Transformation Problem

2.1 The Transformation Problem

At the centre of controversies in Marxist economics has been the so-called transformation problem. Disagreements over its nature and its 'solution' have wide implications, for each treatment of the transformation problem contains a different understanding of Marxist method. These differences in method have to be recognised since, not surprisingly, they are the source of further theoretical differences which at first appear to bear little or no direct relation to the transformation problem as such.

The transformation problem appears to have as its object the transformation of values into prices of production. However, the idea of a 'transformation' has a twofold nature and this is the source of much dispute. On the one hand transformation can be a purely quantitative process, deriving the numerical levels (or ratios) of prices of production by solving a set of simultaneous equations. On the other hand, transformation means a qualitative difference and relationship between value and price of production. Marx, as Baumol (1974) shows, was undoubtedly concerned with both these aspects of transformation, with the qualitative aspect being uppermost, whereas modern neo-Ricardian writers are, as we shall see, exclusively concerned with the quantative aspect: it is a solution based on the capitalist principle of distribution. In volumes I and II are produced the categories of society's total surplus value, S, and total capital advanced, $C+V$, measured as values. The ratio of these categories in the form $S/C+V=r$

21

is the whole of capital's rate of profit *expressed in value terms.* As such, however, the expression relates to the existence of total social capital as capital-in-general, that is rather than as many-capitals in competition with each other. Marx's transformation, though, is and must be located in the context of many capitals in competition; it is an aspect of the problem of how surplus value is distributed between capitals in competition. This problem is resolved by adopting the principle of distribution which exists as a tendency in reality (and which is recognised both by Classical and neo-Classical economics as well), the principle that competing capitals receive an equal rate of profit on capital advanced. Taking it for granted for the moment that profit is a form of surplus value, this implies that capitalists receive a share of total surplus value proportional to the capital they have advanced.

Marx argued, wrongly, that the rate of profit received by each capital was equal to r, the value rate of profit: total surplus value as a percentage of capital as a whole expressed in values. Despite the error of that argument, the principle of distribution at once provides a numerical solution to the transformation problem, a statement of the quantitative relationship between value and price of production.

This can be seen as follows. Suppose social capital comprises two individual capitals of equal value (100). They must, according to the principle of distribution appropriate an equal quantity of surplus value of $r \times 100$. The amount each appropriates, however, does not in general equal the amount of surplus value produced by each. If they use constant and variable capital in different ratios (say 60:40 and 40:60 respectively) then each capital produces a different quantity of surplus value. With a rate of exploitation, s/v, of 100 per cent for example, then the capitals individually produce 40 and 60 surplus value. This means that the average rate of profit in value terms is $r=50$ per cent ($=40+60/60+40+40+60$) and, by Marx's principle of distribution, each capital would appropriate 50 surplus value. This, however, is incompatible with the exchange of commodities at their values so that if the principle of distribution is to hold they must exchange at prices of production which differ from values. The values of the commodities are respectively 140 ($=60c+40v+40s$) and 160 ($=40c+60v+60s$); since $c+v$ in each case equals 100, then, if the commodities exchanged at their values, the (value) rate of profit in one industry would be 40 per cent and in the other 60 per cent. This would contravene the principle of distribution. For the principle to hold the commodities must exchange, according to Marx, at prices of production or modified values defined by marking up each cost of production ($c+v$) by r. In the present example each commodity would have the same price of production, 150.

The *error* in Marx's quantitative transformation (one aspect of which is the idea that the equalised rate of profit equals r, the value rate of total social capital considered as capital-in-general) together with the *strength* of his approach can only be understood in relation to the qualitative aspect of the transformation. In volumes I and II production and then production and exchange are considered in abstraction from distribution. The equalisation-of-profit-rate principle is abstracted from because distribution between competing capitals in different industries is not introduced. Thus, the relevant concepts are values, surplus value, and the value rate of profit. In volume III, however, the preceding analysis of production and exchange is integrated with the theory of distribution between capitals; competing capitals and the principle of distribution are considered in full. This integration means that the concepts must be transformed; values into prices of production (or modified values), surplus value into profit (or modified surplus value), and the value rate of profit into the price of production (or modified value) rate of profit. Significantly, Marx's treatment of these transformations (in particular in the formation and equalisation of the general rate of profit) is conducted on the basis of social capital in existence as many capitals in competition with each other (see Rosdolsky (1977)). For otherwise, the rate of profit could not be formed except as an ideal abstraction derived from production (i.e. the value rate of profit as defined by total social capital as capital-in-general). At times Marx does argue as if the general rate of profit can be constructed from total social capital as capital-in-general, but this is only when he considers (incorrectly) its quantitative formation. In general, it is formed qualitatively in the context of many-capitals in competition, as an averaging rather than aggregate process. Thus, Marx's theory consists of the proposition that this transformation is not an arbitrary, purely mental operation, but parallels the relations of determination which exist in reality. In other words, in reality surplus value is produced but it never appears as such; it appears as profit. Values appear as prices of production (if we abstract from the difference between market prices and prices of production) and these, as we have seen, are formed through competition according to the principle of distribution. They are values modified according to that principle.

Thus Marx's transformation is the production of new concepts in integrating the spheres of production, exchange, and distribution; its 'solution' involves an analysis of the complex unity of production, exchange, and distribution. Any treatment of it that fails to recognise this is bound to be one-sided and incomplete. This gives us a framework in which to analyse Marx's 'solution' to the transformation problem and more recent ones.

The great virtue of Marx's treatment is that it is not one-sided; it does not neglect one or another of production, exchange, or distribution in their unity. Nevertheless, Marx does make an *inadequate* integration of exchange with production and distribution. The integration can be located in terms of the circuit of capital. Examining the sphere of production $C \ldots P \ldots C'$ in abstraction, values and surplus value are, for Marx, the appropriate concepts. But as capital moves out of that sphere *into* the sphere of exchange $(C'-M'-C)$ with which it is integrated together with the distribution sphere, values $(c+v+s)$ are transformed into prices of production $(c+v)(1+r)$. In all this, however, capital advanced is treated as untransformed values; c and v are in terms of values rather than prices of production. It is this which is inadequate. For it implies that capital assumes the price relation as it *comes out* of the sphere of production, that it *enters* the sphere of production as unmodified values, and that it does so by magic. For no consideration is given to the question of how the prices of production are transformed back into values as capital re-enters the sphere of production from exchange. In fact, as Marx recognised but did not work out, as long as we are at the level of abstraction which explicitly involves distribution we should not attempt to consider the transformation of prices of production back into values at the end of $(C'-M'-C)$. Instead, we should work only with prices of production so that capital advanced is $(c'+v')$ rather than $(c+v)$ at *every* point in the circuit of capital: the former is capital expressed in prices of production, the latter is capital expressed in values. This can be put in another way. When commodity-capital is realised (in the movement $C'-M'$), surplus value is redistributed among capitalists and is not appropriated quantitatively in exchange according to the individual processes by which it is created in production. Such is the consequence of differing individual ratios of constant to variable capital. But the redistribution of surplus value between individual capitalists also takes place when capital is advanced to purchase means of production (in the movement $M-C$ *(LP/MP)* by which the form of productive capital is reproduced. As in the movement $C'-M'$, this follows from the exchange of commodities at their prices of production as opposed to their values. It is the movement $C'-M'$ that Marx emphasises at the expense of the movement $M-C$, and it leads to certain errors to which we return below. This Marx recognises, for he observes that the value of capital advanced may diverge from the price of production of that capital, but he makes no effort to correct his discrepancy.

This omission on Marx's part has bred considerable controversy. It has led the neo-Ricardian school to reject value analysis altogether (see, for example, articles by Hodgson and Steedman). As we shall see this is not simply a conclusion of their theory but also their very starting-point. For neo-Ricardianism bases its analysis on the technical relations of production. These comprise the physical and labour inputs necessary to produce any given set of commodities. For example, to produce a given commodity, quantities $x_1, x_2, \ldots x_n$ of certain raw materials (physical means of production) may be necessary as well as a quantity ℓ of labour-time (not labour-power). Now if we impose on these technical conditions of production a system of exchange relations, in which every input has a price, then the cost of producing the commodity in question is simply

$$p_1x_1 + p_2x_2 \ldots + p_nx_n + w\ell,$$

where p_1, p_2 ..., p_i ..., p_n are the prices of the first, second, ..., ith, ... inputs and w is the wage-payment. In so far as this cost is less than the price of the commodity produced, there is room for profit, and this implies the existence of a rate of profit on costs advanced so that

$$p = (p_1x_1 + p_2x_2 \ldots + p_nx_n + w\ell)\,(1 + r'),$$

where p is the price of the commodity and r' the price rate of profit. Clearly r' is a different concept from r, the value rate of profit. Later we shall see that it is also numerically different.

If we assume that the economy is competitive in the sense that the price paid for any input (including labour) is the same for any purchaser and that the rate of profit is the same for the production of any output, then it follows that we can write down similar equations as the one above for every commodity. That is, the price of a commodity is determined by marking up costs of production since each input in the economy (except labour) is considered to be the output of some production process. This means that our technical relations of production generate a system of simultaneous equations. In these, prices in the economy are related to the wage rate and the profit rate. It is the solution of this set of equations which has been the major theoretical object of the neo-Ricardian school.

What they can show is that prices can be eliminated from the equations to leave an inverse relationship between the level of wages and the rate of profit. This is hardly a surprising result and corresponds to the inverse relationship between the value of labour-power and the value rate of profit, when everything else is held constant. It leads neo-Ricardians to conclude that distribution (in particular the rate of profit) in capitalist society is equally determined by economic class struggle for higher wages and the ability of productivity increases (i.e. development of the technical relations of production) to provide for higher wages (Gough (1975)).

This conclusion is deceptively appealing. Indeed, it has an air of tautology about it. It is reinforced by what is considered to be a devastating critique of the errors in Marx's transformation. There are two which are held up as being irredeemable. The first is that Marx, as we have seen, formulated the principle of distribution in terms of equalisation of each industry's rate of profit to the value rate of profit, r, on capital in general. Because of this Marx derives prices of production by marking costs up by $(1+r)$, believing this equivalent to $(1+r')$. The neo-Ricardians easily show that this equivalence is not valid. The price of production rate of profit, r', depends only upon the technical relations of production and the wage rate. Specifically it does not depend on the allocation of capital between industries (the sectoral composition of output). The value rate of profit, however, does depend on the allocation of capital. This rate is expressed as $r = S/C + V = (S/V)/(C/V + 1)$. Since C, V, S, S/V, C/V are aggregate values, C/V is the weighted sum, the average, of each industry's ratio of C/V. If, given S/V, capital moves from one industry to another with a different ratio of c to v the average ratio C/V will change and so will r (unless S/V is zero). This shows that r cannot equal r' except by chance, by a fortuitous allocation of capital, and Marx was mistaken to assume equivalence. The second error which the neo-Ricardians take as damning is the inadequacy we have already examined. Capitalists have to buy labour-power and means of production on the basis of prices of production (as well as sell commodities on this basis). Therefore capital advanced is $(C' + V')$ rather than $(C + V)$ and the prices of the produced commodities should be calculated as $(c' + v')(1 + r')$ rather than $(c + v)(1 + r)$.

The neo-Ricardian critique of Marx's 'errors' in his transformation, however, is not the main element in their critique. Much more fundamental, apparently devastating in fact, is their proposition that even if these 'errors' were corrected Marx's transformation is wrong in the sense that it is unnecessary: the theoretical framework in which Marx poses the transformation problem is wrong. Marx's transformation is superfluous because prices of production and the related concepts of profit can be obtained without any reference to value or surplus value at all. It is an 'irrelevant detour' (see Samuelson (1971)) to start with values and then transform them to prices of production.

This conclusion has at its starting-point the calculation of values from the technical conditions of production. The neo-Ricardian interpretation of value is based on consideration of equations of the type

$$W = W_1 x_1 + W_2 x_2 + \ldots + W_n x_n + \ell,$$

where W is the value of an output produced by the inputs x_1, $\ldots$, x_n which have values $W_1, \ldots, W_n$ and ℓ is the living labour input. To calculate the value of a commodity we add up the dead labour embodied in the physical inputs used to produce it (as measured by their values, W_1, W_2, etc.) together with the quantity of direct living labour. These value equations can be solved to find the labour-time necessary to produce any commodity and this constitutes the neo-Ricardian concept of value. It is simply a measure of labour-time embodied.

What is significant in this procedure is that the technical relations of production are the logical origin of their value equations, just as earlier they were the logical origin of the price equations. This leads the neo-Ricardians to the conclusion that it is quite unnecessary to proceed via values to the determination of prices. In effect the transformation of values into prices is an irrelevant stumbling block, because prices can be calculated directly without any reference to value. Since, for neo-Ricardians, the important object is the theory of prices and since they see their concept of value as unnecessary for this, they conclude by rejecting the relevance of value theory.

Since it appears to have this destructive implication for Marx's value theory, it is not surprising that the neo-Ricardian approach to the transformation problem has been subject to criticism. One line of attack, adopted by Yaffe, is to identify neo-Ricardianism with bourgeois economics because of its preoccupation with prices of production and profit and rejection of value concepts. The two are identified, that is, because the object of analysis for each is never at a more abstract level than that of exchange and distribution. An extreme form of criticism is to argue that neo-Ricardians cannot analyse production. Such a statement is not true; all that is true is that they cannot analyse production in abstraction from exchange and distribution. We shall return to this below (Section 2.2).

Fundamentalists, like neo-Ricardians, approach the transformation problem in such a way that it is impossible to understand its status as the central point in the integration of the three spheres of production, distribution and exchange. As represented by Yaffe (1975) and Howell (1975) their view of the transformation is extremely one-sided, seeing it as a process which relates solely to the sphere of exchange. This is paradoxical for, as we have noted in Chapter 1, the whole point of the Fundamentalists' work in other respects is to emphasise the determining role of production and to neglect the analysis of the sphere of exchange. In what sense, then, do they ignore production in the transformation problem and what is the source of this error? They ignore production in the sense that, as argued by Howell, they think the transformation is from one exchange category to another. The transformation is, in their view, from (values expressed in) prices to prices of production. Paradoxically this arises from an attempt to argue (Yaffe) that Marx's transformation, forming prices of production from costs and profit rate in value terms, is correct because it is founded on value concepts which are relevant to production. The only way the Fundamentalists can reason that input costs and the rate of profit do not have to be themselves transformed (from C, V, r to C', V', r') is on the grounds that they are already price, exchange, categories. In this way they lose precisely the object which they desire; they maintain the proposition that value categories are indispensable, but in doing so they distort the concept of value so that it becomes only an exchange rather than a production category, although this is not realised and Fundamentalists continue to assert the priority of production.

Rowthorn (1973) has made a more extensive criticism of the neo-Ricardian derivation of prices of production. He argues that the neo-Ricardian method leads it to fail to comprehend capitalism as a specific mode of production. The class relations of production are entirely absent from the neo-Ricardian system which depends exclusively upon distributional relations based on property rights. In fact, the neo-Ricardian price equations fail to distinguish a capitalist system of wage-labour from a system in which workers hire machinery for their own use from capitalists by a 'rent' (profit) payment. This failure arises from the neo-Ricardian treatment of labour like any other factor input. This is quite explicit in their cost and mark-up calculations where the labour costs $w\ell$ enter equally with each $p_i x_i$: living labour has the same status as means of production (dead labour). This implies the use of the concept of the price of labour (the wage) and the failure to make the distinction, crucial for Marxism, between labour and labour-power. (It should be noted, however, that Hodgson (1976) claims the opposite, that neo-Ricardianism emphasises the distinction between labour and labour-power whereas other Marxists do not. This claim is quite incomprehensible.)

It is arguments of this sort that Rowthorn uses to criticise the historically ambiguous concept of the capitalist mode of production that is implicit in the neo-Ricardian method. He particularly emphasises the inability of neo-Ricardians to demonstrate the coercive power of capitalists over labour in the production process. It is in production that the classes of capitalist society confront each other on unequal terms. The exclusive preoccupation of neo-Ricardians with exchange gives ideological support to the bourgeoisie, for it is relations of exchange, and not production, that incorporate the bourgeois concept of equality *par excellence*.

Rowthorn's criticisms are significant but limited, as is illustrated by the willingness of the less extreme neo-Ricardians to accept value analysis as a 'sociology of capitalist exploitation'. This reduces Marxism to a moral polemic rather than a science. Value can be seen by neo-Ricardianism as a category that simplifies the explanation of the form of exploitation in capitalist society. Marxism then becomes a sophisticated development of the theory of the natural right of labour. What is denied is that value is a necessary or even useful concept for uncovering the laws of motion of capitalism. This follows from the neo-Ricardian assumption that the necessary objects of analysis for such a study are the price categories that appear in exchange and which they alone calculate correctly.

Interestingly neo-Ricardians have never really justified their view that prices are of such significance. Why is the price (rather than value) rate of profit, for example, a central concept for understanding capitalist development? Their explicit rationale for this is that their rate of profit is the central variable governing the behaviour (i.e. investment) of *individual* capitalists (and consequently capital as a whole), and that this price rate of profit is a central indicator of distributional struggle. These reasons are extemely weak, relying upon an aggregation of individual propensities independent of the coercion of underlying social forces and betraying a limited notion of the role of surplus in capitalist society (an absolute priority to distribution). Nevertheless the neo-Ricardian assertion of the necessity for priority of distribution in the economic analysis of capitalism can only be met in analyses such as Yaffe's and Rowthorn's by the counter-assertion of the priority of production.

The barriers of dogma to which this situation led have begun to be broken down by the simple realisation that capitalist, indeed commodity, production involves a unity of the processes of exchange and production. It is not a case of a theory of production versus a theory of distribution, but a theory of distribution linked to production through exchange. This method can restore the Marxist priority of production in determination but it need not suspend it in isolation from distribution. In this light the neo-Ricardian theory cannot offer an alternative because as we show in Section 2.2 it does not contain a theory of *capitalist* production, the consequence of its rejection of value analysis. Indeed, neo-Ricardianism now appears as a poor imitation not so much of Ricardo as of Mill with the latter's emphasis on the natural laws of production and the socially determined relations of distribution.

The heart of the matter can be seen by considering the concepts of labour which are respectively associated with Marx's and the neo-Ricardian concepts of value. For Marx, the abstract labour which underlies value is a real category produced by capitalist market relations. For as far as capitalist exchange proceeds smoothly the market strips individual types of labour of their individuality (see Arthur (1976) and Kay (1976)) and makes them commensurable as abstract labour; the other side of the same phenomenon is that commodities produced by labour are themselves commensurable and therefore have value and exchange value. This process is one which arises from capitalist market exchange as such and it does not depend upon the equalisation of the rate of profit: it is more fundamental or, to put it another way, it is at a higher level of abstraction. Therefore value itself is at a higher level of abstraction than exchange value (prices of production) for the latter only exist in the context of equalisation of the rate of profit. This, however, is not recognised by neo-Ricardians for their value equations, summing quantities of abstract labour, are considered simply as (redundant) alternatives to price of production equations – alternative accounting systems – and therefore not at different levels of abstraction. Pilling (1972) and Williams (1975) point out that this failure to understand that price of production is a transformed (or 'mediated') form of value was the primary fault in Classical economics which Marx exposed. For price of production to be a form of value a transformation is necessary – one which proceeds from one level of abstraction to another or, in other words, grasps the integration of production, exchange and distribution.

In a major contribution Gerstein (1976) shows the significance of this although he tends to subsume distribution in exchange. His treatment of the transformation problem is related to the solution developed by Seton (1957). Seton's difference from the usual neo-Ricardian approach arises because he does transform values into prices of production even if by reference to the technical relations of production that are so fundamental to neo-Ricardiansim. This is simply done by setting up simultaneous equations between the price rate of profit and the ratios of prices of production to values. This involves correcting Marx's failure to transform the original costs of production from values into prices of production. For the simultaneous equation system determines the prices of commodities as both outputs and inputs. Quantitatively the neo-Ricardian and Seton solutions must coincide, but their interpretation remains quite different. For the former, values are a detour in the derivation of prices and profits from technical relations of production whereas for the latter values are the starting point. Seton's solution can be seen as representing the unity of production, exchange and distribution. Value categories enter *ab initio*, and the transformation explicitly constructs modified values based on this unity.

Gerstein's analysis of the integration of the production and exchange of values leads to his insistence that Seton's procedure is incomplete. This is because his solution to the transformation problem is only unique up to scale – it determines relative prices of production, the ratios of the prices of different commodities, and not absolute levels. This is a property in common with the neo-Ricardian determination of prices. Starting from a given wage level (corresponding to a given bundle of wage goods) prices of commodities are deduced. If we had set the wage level differently (for the same bundle of wage goods) then the level of prices would be correspondingly higher. There appears to be no rationale for choosing one *level* of price rather than another. This is because the integration of production and distribution only requires a calculation of the *relative* shares appropriated by capital and labour. Gerstein, however, characterises the choice of the absolute level of prices as the central factor forging the link between the production and circulation of value. He argues that this requires a level of prices for which total value equals total price (rather than one where total surplus value equals total profit, which in general is incompatible with the other condition).

While Gerstein is correct to emphasise the transformation of values into prices of production as an integration of production and exchange, this does not depend ultimately upon choosing an appropriate absolute level of prices. Indeed, the development of such an absolute level of prices is quite meaningless without the existence of a general equivalent, i.e. money, and the direct intervention of money in the exchange process has been correctly absent from the analysis of the transformation. We have been treating value and surplus value as they exist in exchange but not explicitly as they exist in money form (except as an expositional device above on page 24). At a lower level of abstraction, in moving from prices of production to money prices, i.e. from the circulation of (modified) values to the circulation of money, it will be necessary to relate the modified values of commodities to the modified value of commodity-money. Further development of the concept of market price depends upon the concept of fiat money and analysis of the credit system.

Before leaving the transformation problem it is worth noting that its relevance is by no means confined to formal, logical issues which have no bearing on class struggle. Failure to see the transformation in terms of the complex unity of production, exchange and distribution is linked to particular views of class struggle. We shall see in later chapters that the neo-Ricardian concern with exchange leads them to see the class struggles associated with crises as essentially struggles over wages and profits (exchange categories) rather than seeing all contradictions as dependent on contradictions in the sphere of production. Equally, the Fundamentalists' concern to emphasise the correctness of Marx's failure to transform $(C+V)$ leads to one-sided conclusions in analysing crises.

2.2   Production and the Significance of Value Theory

We have seen that the most significant conclusion which neo-Ricardians draw from their solution to the transformation problem is that it is a non-problem. There is no need to transform values into prices of production since either is directly derivable from technical relations of production and therefore values are redundant in the determination of prices. By contrast, Fundamentalists have emphasised the importance of values which are in no sense made redundant by the existence of prices of production. In the present Section we consider why value is indispensable in the analysis of capitalism.

We have already argued in Section 2.1 that the existence of values and their transformation into prices is the same as the existence of production in abstraction and its integration with exchange and distribution. The rejection of value theory, therefore, is the same as the rejection of Marx's method; the method of moving from the most simple abstract relations to the most complex. Now, however, we must do more than demonstrate that value theory is essential to Marx's method. Hodgson (1977) has challenged Marxists to show that production cannot be analysed without value theory.

The challenge is difficult to pin down for it can have several meanings. At the simplest level it is a request for a demonstration that capitalist production cannot be analysed in terms of prices of production. At that level, neo-Ricardianism is successful since production can be analysed in those terms; phenomena such as the length of the working day can be studied by assuming that capitalists are driven to maximise profit (in terms of prices of production) rather than surplus value. Indeed, Steedman (1977) provides such an analysis. But the neo-Ricardian ability to carry out such an analysis is trivial. A theory of a determinate length of the working day can be derived, in bourgeois terms, by postulating any maximand for capitalists to obey; profits in terms of market prices as in neo-classical theory, or management objectives as in managerial theories of the firm. There is therefore nothing surprising about the fact that determinate production decisions by capitalists can be deduced from a maximand in terms of profit measured in prices of production.

At another level it is a request for a proof that values exist, but as such it is an impossible request. For one thing, as Pilling (1972) notes, Marx himself dismissed the challenge to prove the existence of value and thought it more important to work out the effects of its existence. For another, the idea of proof is a source of extreme controversy among Marxists and the request for a proof can hardly be met without some agreement as to what would constitute one.

But we can go a long way toward demonstrating the superiority of Marx's theory founded on value theory over theories which abandon values by enumerating the specific results obtained by employing value theory. The essential point is that value theory is necessary for the analysis of production *while abstracting from* exchange and distribution; this cannot be done using price categories since these are only relevant on the basis of an integrated structure of production, exchange, and distribution with competition within and between industries. The question therefore is what specific results are obtained by analysing production in abstraction.

There are three conclusions reached by Marx which are especially significant in distinguishing his work from Classical and neo-Classical political economy and which are uniquely based on this abstraction. First, the determining contradiction in capitalism is the antagonism of the two great classes; second, capitalism is a dynamic system producing constant revolutions in the process of production; third, capitalism involves tensions and displacements between production, exchange and distribution. In the following three paragraphs we look at each in turn. In each case it is easy to see that the conclusion can only be based upon the abstract analysis of production, and that this abstract analysis conforms to the method of constructing the structure of abstraction and determination outlined in the previous chapter.

The antagonism of the bourgeoisie and proletariat is founded upon the antagonism of capital and labour. This involves an undifferentiated concept of capital as well as of labour (viz. abstract labour). It is the struggle of capital-in-general with labour-in-general which is at the root of capitalism's reproduction and the limits to it. The struggle of many-capitals in competition with each other through exchange does not have the same significance. Taking the struggle of capital-in-general as basic, it is logically impossible to analyse it in terms of prices which differ from values, for such prices only exist on the basis of competitive exchange between many capitals (equalisation of the rate of profit). Thus, the analysis of production so that it identifies this struggle must be in terms of values. Moreover, this value analysis does not involve ignoring exchange until a later stage of analysis. Marx's value analysis is explicitly applied to exchange but, as with production, it concerns only exchange between *capital* and *labour* – the purchase of labour-power as a commodity being an indispensable fact – rather than exchange between capitals. Thus, when it is stated that value analysis abstracts from exchange this means abstraction from the complexities of exchange which result from competitive exchange between capitals.

The dynamic nature of capitalism – in the sense of the

introduction of new techniques of production – is similarly seen as being fundamentally based on the antagonism of capital-in-general with labour. As such it can, again, logically only be analysed in value terms. With the concept of relative surplus value Marxism demonstrates that the essential property of capital-in-general – self-expansion – must involve technical change. Moreover, even when we go beyond the properties of capital-in-general and consider how competition between capitals forces innovations we do not immediately enter a realm where prices of production are relevant. For, as Marx argues, the form of competition relevant to this process is that between capitals *within* each particular industry. It is a question of how each capital within the industry attempts to gain a larger amount of surplus value by expelling living labour. For this within-industry analysis only values are relevant; prices of production exist and are relevant only in the context of exchange and competition across industries.

That tensions and displacements between production, exchange, and distribution exist is a fact which is central to Marxist analyses of crises and cycles. For example, the existence of speculative booms preceding crises is an aspect of the over-expansion of exchange in relation to production, and this over-expansion may be precipitated by *distributional* struggle between capital and labour and between individual capitals. It is, however, based upon the fundamental contradiction of capitalist *production* – that between capital and labour over the production of surplus value. In order to study these relationships between the spheres it is necessary to study their articulation. And it is not possible to study the articulation between production, exchange and distribution and their displacements unless we have a concept of them as distinct spheres unified in a hierarchical relation; unless, that is, we can consider the determining sphere, production, in abstraction.

There are, then, three particular results obtained by Marx on the basis of value analysis. Neo-Ricardianism, by abandoning such analysis, cannot obtain these results although it may in some cases put forward propositions which appear similar. The articulation between spheres with its tensions and displacements is explicitly abandoned in favour of analysis based on the existence of a simple (hence harmonious) unity between spheres. The dynamic of capitalism is treated as determined by distributional struggle over exchange relations (wages and profits) instead of as dependent upon the class relations of production. This choice of exchange relations as the objects of analysis is in a sense arbitrary, since if the economy is seen as a simple unity any aspect of it can be chosen as 'representing' the whole. The analysis of production as a relation between capital-in-general and labour (with associated exchange relations between these categories) is abandoned in favour of a study of production with many-capitals which are in competition with each other through mutual exchange.

These paragraphs indicate why value analysis is essential for the study of capitalism. It is not a question of its necessity for analysing production in some general sense, but of analysing production in its complex unity with exchange and distribution. The existence of value cannot be ignored if we are to distinguish the specifically capitalist order of determination and articulation between the spheres of economic life. This brings us to another contentious point concerning neo-Ricardianism. Writers such as Rowthorn (1973) have criticised the neo-Ricardian system on the grounds that it is ahistorical. The theory is, it is said, as applicable to a society of petty commodity producers as it is to capitalism. Hodgson (1977), however, rejects these criticisms. He argues, quite rightly, that neo-Ricardianism takes as central a feature specific to capitalism, the price system which results from the capitalist equalisation of the rate of profit across industries. In this sense, therefore, the neo-Ricardian system is specific to capitalism. It is, however, ahistorical in the sense that the equalisation of the rate of profit is not the determinant aspect of the capitalist economic process. The determinant aspect is the struggle between capital-in-general and labour; and this, as we have seen, cannot be analysed in the neo-Ricardian system. Without it the struggle of the two great classes under capitalism becomes non-analysable as such and merely a struggle linked to and of the same status as the struggle between individual capitalists. Indeed it can be argued (see

Fine (1975*b*) and Fine and Harris (1977)) that the neo-Ricardian analysis of economic reproduction on the basis of individual competition (between capitalists) leads logically to a theory which also includes individual competition between workers, that is ultimately to neo-Classical theory. It is this inability to comprehend the principal contradiction of capitalism that makes neo-Ricardianism ahistorical.

2.3 Joint Production and Fixed Capital

In this chapter we have seen that neo-Ricardians reject value theory on the grounds that it is redundant. They also consider that because of the existence of joint production, not only is Marx's value theory redundant but also its claim to analyse the source of profit is unfounded. This according to Steedman (1975) (1976) is a further reason for rejecting Marx's value theory. The argument that Marx's value theory cannot ana-lyse the source of profit is based on the idea that when joint production exists positive profit may be accompanied by negative surplus value (Steedman (1975) (1976), Hodgson (1977)). Thus what Morishima (1973) calls the Fundamental Marxian Theorem, that a necessary condition for positive profit is positive surplus value, is found to be invalid. We shall see that this conclusion is based upon a particular concept of value and surplus value, and it is not one which is consistent with Marx's problematic. We begin by explaining how the problem arises within the neo-Ricardian framework.

Joint production means the creation of more than one product from a single production process. A classic example is cattle rearing. The process of rearing, killing, then skinning cattle results in two products – carcasses (which are then processed into meat) and hides (which may be processed into leather). Another is the process of producing gas from coal: two products result from the single process, gas and coke. But for the neo-Ricardians the most important example, because it is thought to be the most pervasive, is the case of fixed capital. Fixed capital takes the form of machines and other means of production which are not wholly consumed by the production process in a single production period. In conse-quence any production process which employs fixed capital produces two products. One is the commodity which the production process is designed to produce, the other is 'old machinery.' That is, taking the production period as a 'year' the product includes means of production 'machinery' which is one year older than it was when the process was initiated. This is taken to be a joint product.

How does Steedman (1975) reason that joint production leads to the possibility of positive profits with negative surplus value? Bearing in mind that surplus value is calculated in terms of values (and qualitatively both are at the same level of abstraction) while profit is in terms of prices of production, the possibility arises because joint production may cause some commodities to have negative values while they have positive prices. This way of presenting it suggests that the problem is purely one of arithmetic – how to divide up a given quantity of labour so that one of its products embodies a quantity greater than the total. Steedman (1975) presents a numerical example along these lines. The argument is that all commodities have positive prices because they are by definition useful; they command a price as use values. But how can a commodity have negative value? If there is no joint production the possibility does not arise. Each commodity is uniquely produced by a single process and its value is the living and dead labour expended therein. But suppose there are two commodities. One is produced with itself alone as physical input in combination with living labour (say corn which is simply sown and reaped). As a result corn has a value determined by the ratio of living labour to *net* output. In addition, corn may be used to produce itself and another product (say, pigeons which are attracted by the corn but captured by hand without loss of corn). For this second production process the value embodied is simply the quantity of living labour expended together with the value of constant capital which is the value of corn (previously determined) multiplied by the quantity used. Now the value of output is the sum of the value of the corn produced (which is known) and the value of the pigeons produced. It is possible that the former *exceeds* the value embodied in the production process, so that this can only be equal to the value of output produced if pigeons (or at least their production) unwittingly have a negative value! Essentially what has happened is that the *extra* labour exerted to produce pigeons has simultaneously increased the output of corn (no losses to pigeons) so that the value of outputs exceeds the value of inputs unless pigeons are negatively valued.

From this several things are immediately apparent. First, the problem arises because a particular allocation rule is employed for calculating the values of the individual commodities. We shall see that Steedman (1975) (1976) uses one allocation rule whereas Morishima (1974) (1976) and Catephores and Morishima (1978) use a different allocation rule and find that positive profit only exists if surplus value is positive. Second, the problem is presented as purely one of arithmetic. The important question, though, is whether joint production should be presented as a mathematical problem in this way or whether doing so involves a concept of value different from Marx's. Third, the problem is based on a particular definition of joint production, the one employed by Sraffa (1960), represented by the simple idea of a production process. With one or more means of production plus labour more than one commodity is produced, each of which has a price. For the case of two inputs and two outputs the price equation describing the process is:

$$(p_1x_1+p_2x_2+w\ell)\,(1+r')=p_1x_1+p_2x_2.$$

Each of these three characteristics of Steedman's proof of the possibility of negative values is problematical. The problem with his concept of a process, his Sraffian concept that if x_1 and x_2 have use value they must have a price, and also the problem with his treatment of value as an arithmetical property, are both most evident in the case which the neo-Ricardians take to be most significant. This is where a process has two products, the commodity for which it is designed and an 'old machine'. For Marx values are only carried by products (by use-values) if they are commodities; although value is not the same as exchange it is the commodity's existence as an object produced for exchange which gives it value. The 'old machine' however, is not in principle produced for exchange, it is not a commodity. Although markets in second-hand machinery do exist they are not essential to the capitalist production process: instead, 'old machines' in general re-enter the production process each period without being exchanged. In this case, therefore, the operation of allocating (negative or positive) labour time to an 'old machine' is a purely ideal operation which bears no relation to the Marxist concept of value since it is divorced from the material circumstance that old machines are not commodities. The neo-Ricardian allocation of labour-time is not the same as the conceptualisation of values; to put it another way, the neo-Ricardians assume that simply because the 'old machine' exists and has a use value it must have a price (as in the above equation) and therefore they equate commodities with use values.

This criticism, although significant because the general existence of fixed capital leads neo-Ricardians to claim that joint production is the general case, does not dispose of the neo-Ricardian argument. There may be other, less pervasive, joint production processes where both products *are* commodities. Steedman's conclusion that in such cases negative values and surplus value may exist with positive profit is contested by Morishima (1974) (1976), Catephores and Morishima (1978) and Wolfstetter (1976). What these writers show is that the particular allocation rule employed by Steedman is responsible for the finding of negative values. Neither side in the debate employs Marx's concept of value, as we shall see, but the debate is of interest in its own right.

Steedman's rule for allocating labour between joint products and calling them values is one which he claims to be Marx's. It is that the sum of the values of the two joint products must equal the labour expended in their production. Associated with this is the rule that the labour expended is that which occurs throughout the particular industry even if several processes of differing efficiency are used in the industry; and, Steedman argues, in general more than one process will be used. Thus, in the industry producing joint products x_1 and x_2 and using x_1 and x_2 as inputs, there will in general be several different processes employed; each process will employ x_1 and x_2 as inputs in different proportions, and each will be used because otherwise expanded reproduction would in general be impossible without disproportionalities. The labour to be allocated to each commodity is the total expended in the industry, even including that in the least efficient process. He argues that this is quantitatively equivalent to Marx's concept of value; an average over all techniques which are used. Morishima's alternative rule, under which negative surplus value with positive profit is impossible, is to calculate values on the basis of labour expended in the most efficient process alone. By 'efficient' is meant those processes which would minimise the direct and indirect (i.e. total) labour-time necessary to produce a given bundle of commodities. What Morishima shows is that this definition of values yields positive ones only, but that values are not additive in the sense that the value (minimum necessary labour-time to produce) of x_1 added to the value of x_2 does not always equal (is in fact less than or equal to) the value of the bundle comprising of x_1 *and* x_2. (For those versèd in these matters, value for Morishima is the shadow price found from the dual of a linear programme, the criterion function of which is to minimise total labour expended.) This is because, with joint production, the labour-time used at a minimum to produce x_1 (or alternatively x_2) may also have as a result some ouput of $x_2(x_1)$, which has to be thrown away in the exercise of producing x_1 alone with minimum labour-time. In terms of our earlier example, it can be shown that the corn production process which does not jointly produce pigeons is inefficient in Morishima's terms and would never occur in the solution to the minimisation of the labour-time necessary to produce any combination of corn and pigeon. If corn alone is required value is formed by adopting the alternative process which produces both corn and pigeons and throwing away the pigeons. But if both are required no extra labour-time is necessary. More generally Morishima has shown that Steedman's negative values can only occur if joint production processes are utilised which prevent labour-time from being minimised, which for Morishima is inefficiency. (It should be borne in mind that Steedman's processes are not unprofitable relative to the efficient, since they can be minimising costs – in value terms $C+V$ – if not total labour-time – $C+V+S$. See below.) Catephores and Morishima (1978) argue in places that this allocation rule is similar to Marx's in that it is based on the idea that the value of a commodity is determined by the labour expended in the most efficient production processes, the ones which employ in total the minimum of labour.

One element of the dispute between Morishima and Steedman, therefore, is the question of which concept of value is most 'close' to that of Marx. Steedman argues that his values are since they correspond, as a result of their additivity, to average labour-time. Morishima in contrast bases his claim on the minimisation of labour-time. In fact, both sides are wrong to claim that their concept of value is close to Marx's. In the case of Steedman, Marx only refers to averaging when capitals are producing at different price rates of profit, when each capitalist has not adopted the least costly technique. Steedman, in contrast, averages over techniques which do have rates of profit equalised by competition. For Marx, leaving aside the problem of joint production, this is to be associated with a commonly adopted technique for which no averaging is therefore necessary. Consequently Steedman's interpretation of Marx's concept of value is flawed by a conflation of levels of abstraction. His own analysis is conducted at that level which includes prices of production and for which profit rates are equalised; competition has 'worked itself out.' His interpretation of Marx is at that level for which averaging is necessary and which therefore precludes the establishment of prices of production through profit equalisation. This misunderstanding of Marx by Steedman is a product of the neo-Ricardian rejection of the levels of abstraction to be found in *Capital* and a reliance upon a simple unity of economic relations.

This does not, however, mean that Morishima's concept of value is close to Marx's, even though the former does calculate values by assuming that only efficient techniques are employed. The reason for this is that Morishima's 'values' are a purely ideal accounting concept (as are Steedman's) and, related to this, his concept of efficiency differs from Marx's. For Marx, value has a real existence; and the socially necessary labour-time which is its basis is actually determined by the forces of competition which cause inefficient techniques to be abandoned. As Marx makes clear, this competitive minimisation of costs concerns not total labour alone but living and dead labour combined as *capital* for which surplus labour remains unpaid. Morishima's values on the other hand are derived by assuming the minimisation of total labour. Thus, the real competition which Marx sees as the basis of value forces profit maximisation but this is not the same as Morishima's minimisation of labour time. Indeed, Marx makes it clear that Morishima's values correspond to a communist as opposed to a capitalist economy (see *Capital*, vol. I, p. 371).

Thus, neither Steedman nor Morishima employ Marx's concept of value. The most fundamental divergence from Marx's concept in both cases is that each writer sees value simply as an accounting concept whereas Marx treats it as a real phenomenon which has concrete effects. But it is one thing to show that the values employed by Morishima and Steedman are not Marx's. It is another to discuss how Marx's value system is affected by the existence of joint products. Remembering that for Marx values have real effects in determining production techniques (being, as we saw in section 2.2, the basis of within-industry competition) it is pertinent to ask not only what is the effect of joint production on values, but what is the effect of values on joint production. It will be seen that the answer to the second question has an effect on the first. It is that the existence of values under capitalism, hence the organisation of production so that it is production of surplus value, gives rise to a tendency toward specialisation. In other words Marx showed on the basis of value theory that there is a tendency toward increased social division of labour. This should apply to joint production itself, leading to the development and adoption of specialised processes. It is wrong of neo-Ricardians to see joint production as being determined by natural technological facts. Instead, technology is the result of, as well as the basis for, social relations (there is a dialectical relationship between forces and relations of production) and its determination results from the production of surplus value. Take the most famous example of joint production. It is wrong of neo-Ricardians to see the joint production of wool and mutton by sheep (means of production) and shepherd as being determined by the nature of sheep and the inseparable nature of the labour process (shepherding). In fact the search for surplus value by capitalist farmers forces a specialisation of processes. Some sheep are bred for mutton, others for wool; new types of sheep are bred which specialise in one or the other and the labour process associated with each is entirely different. This illustration makes clear the meaning of a tendency for joint products to become produced by separate processes and drives home the fact that where joint production exists it is socially rather than technologically determined, according to the development of the combination and division of labour. Consider, in addition, our earlier example of corn and pigeon production. For Steedman and Morishima this involves simply a relation between values and technical conditions. But it is of some significance whether the joint production process is or is not organised by a single capitalist. Indeed in the latter case, in which one capitalist employs workers to produce corn and another to catch pigeons, joint production does not occur and values can be defined in the normal way (although *socially* there is joint production – in common parlance, an externality: for the pigeon producer the social conditions of production vary as corn is or is not produced and vice versa). Nothing illustrates better that the neo-Ricardians commitment to 'logical' questions conceals a subordination of consideration of the organisation and development of production to a preoccupation with supposedly neutral and exogenously determined technical conditions.

But what is the implication of this for Marxist value theory? It remains the case that joint production processes may be chosen by capitalists. To the extent that they are chosen (generalised rather than specialised sheep are bred) competition within the industry is determined by the value of the composite commodity (mutton/wool) which is produced. There is no need for values to be calculated for each individual commodity (mutton and wool separately) in order to analyse this within-industry competition, hence there is no possibility of negative value arising. It is therefore possible to employ value theory to analyse that competition which arises in the sphere of production in abstraction, without separable additive values. But is it possible to examine the integration of the sphere of production with exchange and distribution without such values? Steedman appears to believe that Marx's concept requires separable additive values for this purpose since prices of production are separable and additive. In fact, however, this is not a requirement. Prices of production are, qualitatively, a form of value. If value only exists for composite commodities whereas prices, exchange values, exist for their components, this is only a reflection of the fact that exchange forces labour, inseparable in the sphere of production, into a form which is separable in the sphere of exchange.

Is anything in Marx's value theory lost by treating the value of a composite commodity as non-separable into the values of the joint products which comprise it? The answer is in the negative. To explain why, it is necessary to distinguish two levels of abstraction. Consider first that level where competition between industries is abstracted from the level which pertains to volumes I and II of *Capital*. At this level values are equal to exchange values. The great achievement of value theory, its grasp of the contradiction between labour and capital in production, is maintained as a result. This may not be apparent, for it may be said that if there is a joint process producing two commodities, one a wage good and the other a means of production, it would be impossible to form the value rate of profit, the (value) rate of exploitation, or the value composition of capital since it would be impossible to separate the value of the wage good from that of the means of production. At this level of abstraction, however, it is possible to make this separation and it must be the case that all values of the individual commodities are positive. For the equality of value and exchange value which exists at this level ensures that the process of exchange which allocates positive exchange values forces the value of each commodity in production to be positive. For commodities would not be produced if their exchange value were negative; and at this level of abstraction this is equivalent to making positive value a condition of their production.

Second, consider the lower level of abstraction within which the transformation problem arises. At this level, competition between industries produces equalisation of the rate of profit and the formation of prices of production. Here, because exchange values (prices of production) do not equal values the process of exchange does not guarantee the existence of (positive) values for individual commodities. If at this level of abstraction we restrict the concept of value to composite commodities in the case of joint production, we are still able to grasp the articulation of production, exchange, and distribution in the same manner as did Marx in the absence of joint production. Qualitatively, as we have seen, prices of production remain the form of expression of values even though the former are separable whereas the latter are not. Quantitatively the solution to the transformation problem is the same as that adopted above (Section 2.1). The factors of proportionality for which we solve would, in the case of joint production, relate the price of production of the composite commodity (an average of the individual prices of the joint products) to its value (which does not consist of additive components).

At this level we can analyse competition between industries since in Marx's analysis it is conducted in terms of prices of production and we have seen that they exist. Moreover, this type of competition enables us to study the processes which determine whether joint production exists, the tendency toward specialisation. For if capital moves out of joint production into specialised techniques it is essentially moving from one industry (the mutton/wool industry) to another (either the mutton or the wool industry) and this inter-industry competition depends on prices of production and r'.

3

Productive and Unproductive Labour

3.1 Neo-Ricardian Theories

We have seen in the last chapter that the positions of neo-Ricardians and Fundamentalists on value theory are strongly opposed and that each in its own way fails to take full account of the hierarchical, articulated structure of economic spheres with production determinant. The same characteristics are found in the debate on the nature of productive and unproductive labour, but for the following reason this debate has been conducted with an even greater intensity and has been more at the centre of political debate. The importance of the distinction between the two categories of labour lies in the increasing significance in modern capitalism of those workers who might be classified as unproductive (e.g. state and commerical as opposed to industrial employees). Unproductive employees are not only distinct in the economic functions they perform for capital, but they are increasingly drawn into and hence hold a distinct position in economic, political and ideological class struggle. It is the movement towards an understanding of their role in these struggles and in capitalist society as a whole that makes the clarification of the concept of unproductive labour so potentially fruitful.

In an article that was the starting point for the debate, Gough (1972) summarised (the neo-Ricardian interpretation of) Marx's theory of productive labour:

> To conclude, productive labour is labour exchanged with capital to produce surplus value. As a necessary condition it

must be useful labour, must produce or modify a use-value – increasingly in a collective fashion; that is, it must be employed in the process of production. Labour in the process of circulation does not produce use-values, therefore cannot add to value or surplus value. It does not add to the production of use-values because it arises specifically with commodity production out of the problems of realising the value of commodities. Alongside this group of unproductive labourers are all workers supported directly out of revenue, whether retainers or state employees. This group differs from circulation workers, however, in that they do produce use-values – all public teachers, doctors, etc. would be included in this category today.

The neo-Ricardian school then proceeds to reject this theory, most clearly in Harrison (1973*a*) and Gough and Harrison (1975). The crucial differences between productive and unproductive labour are rejected and the similarities between the positions of all workers are emphasised. The clearest expression of this approach concerns the role of commercial workers (workers 'in the process of circulation'). Whereas Marx's distinction takes as central the proposition that commercial workers are unproductive because they do not produce surplus value, the neo-Ricardians, with their rejection of value categories as the basis for prices and profit, argue that the price rate of profit, r', is determined by the capital advanced in the process of circulation, by merchant's capital (or the wages and cost of means of production advanced in shops, sales offices etc.), on a footing equal to the value of capital advanced in the sphere of production (and so are prices of production and wages). Not only is the capital advanced in the sphere of circulation treated as a determinant of the rate of profit, but also the fact that commercial workers are wage workers who perform unpaid labour is treated as a source of profit. This differs from Marx in that he saw profit as a form of surplus value and the latter is not produced by commercial workers: for him the fact that merchant capitalists obtain profit comes not because their workers are a source of profit but because, whether performing unpaid labour or not, they enable the merchant capitalists to obtain a portion of surplus value whose source is in the sphere of production. If merchant capital had no need of commercial workers there would, in Marx's framework, be no less profit for capital as a whole. It is simply that a larger share than otherwise would go to industrial capitalists. Finally, neo-Ricardians emphasise that the labour process of commercial workers is under the control of capitalists so that, due to the coercive force of competition, there is constant pressure to reduce socially necessary labour-time and expel living labour.

Before proceeding to examine the neo-Ricardian treatment of other categories of workers we should appraise their treatment of commercial workers; the view that the relations of production under which they work are 'materially identical' to those of Marx's productive workers. In doing so, it should be remembered that for Marx the fundamental significance of the distinction was as an aspect of the dependence of all economic processes upon the sphere of production (see Fine (1973)) and in the case of exchange (commercial workers) this dependence was seen at its sharpest. Now the first point to note about the neo-Ricardian rejection of this distinction is that it conforms to the conclusions they draw from the transformation problem. We have seen that there they fail to recognise that the economy is structured as an articulation of distinct but unified spheres of activity, that the sphere of production is determinant, and that the process of abstraction must reflect this. Instead, the different spheres of the economy are collapsed into a simple unity. Precisely the same approach is taken to the present problem, and it not only reflects the approach to the transformation, it uses the conclusions derived therefrom. That is, it concentrates upon commercial workers' (and merchant capital's) contribution to the formation of prices of production and the price rate of profit, ignoring values and surplus value as is dictated by their solution of the transformation. The second point, which is related to this, is that by ignoring the fact that industrial workers produce surplus value whereas commercial workers do not, the neo-Ricardian treatment leads to the conclusion that production and exchange are equally subject to the same laws of motion. They therefore lose the ability to analyse the phenomena which, as we saw in Section 2.2, value theory enabled Marx to analyse: the tensions and displacements between the spheres as accumulation proceeds. They lose the concept of the relatively independent movement of exchange in its dependence upon the laws of production (the 'law of value'). They reinforce this view of non-independence by emphasising that, being under the control of capital, the labour process in both spheres is subject to the same coercive forces of competition; and that in consequence merchants' capital and industrial capital are both subject to laws such as those of concentration and centralisation. However true this is, (and it leaves aside the structural significance of interest-bearing capital as a lever of competition that confronts capital as a whole), it is not strictly relevant. For merchant and industrial capital are reduced to being simply different sectors of the economy, one of which produces the use-value of sale (as opposed to the transformation of the commodity in exchange) while the other produces the actual use-values. (See Fine (1973).) It follows logically that crises and recessions cannot be treated as a disjuncture between the spheres of production and exchange in which the contradictions of the former are expressed and formed in the latter (on which see subsequent chapters). Rather, all that can be involved is a disproportionality between the two 'sectors' of the economy.

The question of the status of commercial workers, however, is not the one which has brought the debate to its current prominence. More interesting is the fact that neo-Ricardianism also treats state employees such as teachers, nurses, and social workers as essentially no different from productive workers. A particularly clear example of this is Gough (1975) which we have criticised elsewhere (Fine and Harris (1976a)). First, for this category of workers the neo-Ricardians again argue that because they are wage labourers they work under materially identical conditions to industrial workers. Here their argument is quite incorrect for the essential point about state employees (exluding those in nationalised industries) is that their labour is not directly under the control of capital and is not directly subject to the coercive force of competition. Often they do not produce use-values with even the price form of the commodity. Second, Gough argues that state employees are essentially productive because they perform surplus labour, and this surplus labour is transformed into surplus value and thence profit. The idea of surplus value as an intermediate step in reaching profit is, as we have seen, an unnecessary diversion for neo-Ricardianism. But since Gough does take this route we can show how his neo-Ricardian concept of value differs from Marx's. For Marx, value and surplus value can only be produced by capital: for Gough they can be produced without capital controlling the labour process. In his scheme the capitalist state (which is not itself capital) can ensure the performance of surplus *labour* and this somehow becomes converted into surplus *value* which is simply appropriated by capital even though not produced under its control. Capital's role is simply to convert surplus labour performed outside its direct control into surplus value, and then appropriate it. If we adopt Marx's approach and deny the possibility of surplus value originating anywhere except in the process of production directly under capital's control then we have to reject Gough's idea that state employees do perform surplus labour, which then takes the form of surplus value; we have to deny the proposition that in this respect they are essentially the same as productive labourers.

It should be emphasised that the issue at stake in the categorisation of state employees is not whether they perform a useful function for capital. There can be no doubt that they do, and so, of course, do commercial workers. The point is that they do not directly produce surplus value, they therefore constitute unproductive labour and their usefulness for capital stems solely from their 'indirect' role, their role in the processes which support but are ultimately dependent upon the production of surplus value by productive labour. Gough's neo-Ricardian categorisation, by contrast, treats this indirect supportive function as if it were itself identical with the production of surplus value. As such it demonstrates that the neo-Ricardian concept of value has within it the basis for freeing itself from a connection with the capitalist mode of production (a connection that, in its treatment of the transformation problem only exists through its consideration of exchange). The better then is it able to rely upon an ahistorical concept of surplus value drawn from a concept of undifferentiated surplus labour (commercial workers, state employees and subsequently domestic labour as in Harrison (1973*b*), and Gough and Harrison (1975)).

3.2   Fundamentalist Theories

Against the neo-Ricardians, Fundamentalists argue that the productive/unproductive distinction cannot be dissolved and, indeed, that political struggle will be led in false directions unless its theory is based on an understanding of the distinction. However, their dichotomy is different from Marx's and controversial in two respects: the cases of luxury production and of state employees in welfare services.

The problem with luxury production (Department III industries) is best illustrated by the work of Bullock (1973) (1974). Basing himself exclusively within the sphere of production he attempts to define as productive that labour which creates surplus value in a form that can be accumulated. This includes produced means of production and wage-goods (which can be exchanged against labour-power) but excludes luxury production. This places him in some embarrassment, because this definition of productive labour differs from Marx's (which includes luxury production). Bullock attempts to compensate for this by arguing that his definition is consistent with Marx's on (nebulous) methodological grounds. Appealing to the movement of theory between levels of abstraction, he considers that at the first level of abstraction, in simply elaborating the production of surplus value, luxury production does embody productive labour, and this is why Marx included this sector in the productive category. But at a lower level of abstraction, accumulation of surplus value is determinant: and since luxury goods cannot be accumulated, he argues that the concept of productive labour must be modified to reflect this. This total emphasis on accumulation accompanied by a lack of clarity, a few terminological errors and a shifting of his position, yield to the neo-Ricardians a field-day of criticism.

In fact, in later work (Bullock and Yaffe (1975)) the criterion of its contribution to accumulation has been dropped as the basis for categorising any particular labour. The criterion becomes simply that of whether labour produces surplus value, and therefore luxury production comes to be counted as productive since workers there do directly produce surplus value. This reformulation is more consistent with Marx's treatment of luxuries.

On the question of state employees in welfare industries, however, Bullock and Yaffe (1975) and Howell (1975) adopt a view which is not consistent with Marx's emphasis on the direct production of surplus value by productive labour. They argue that wage-labour which educates and medically cares for the working class is productive even if it is employed by the state instead of capital and therefore not directly productive of surplus value. They justify this by drawing an analogy between repair work on fixed capital and 'repair' and reproduction of the commodity labour-power. Because Marx categorises machine-repair as productive labour *sui generis*, it is argued that wage-labour reproducing the labourer is also of this genus and hence productive. This is not Marx's theory: for him repair work is not productive because it is of a unique type, but because it is undertaken by industrial capital. However, the error is, like the original error regarding luxuries, symptomatic of a method confined to analysis of production, leading to a definition of productive labour according to the potential and contribution created for accumulation.

Bullock and Yaffe do not recognise that their classification of medical and education workers is different from Marx's. On the contrary, they write that like themselves Marx in *Theories of Surplus Value*, Part I (pp. 167–8), regards as productive labour that which 'produces, trains, develops, maintains or reproduces labour power itself', (except where this labour-power itself is in unproductive employment). Examination of Marx's text, however, makes clear that Marx does *not* classify this labour as productive. When we turn to the relevant quotation we find that Marx is talking about Adam Smith and his first approach to the problem. He immediately adds: 'Smith excludes the latter from his category of productive labour; arbitrarily, but with a certain correct instinct . . . . that if he included it, this would open the flood gates for false pretensions to the title of productive labour.'

3.3   Significance of the Debate

Marx's distinction between productive and unproductive labour is, in fact, one which is simple to understand. If labour directly produces surplus value it is productive; if not, it is unproductive. This criterion has the corollary that only labour which is performed under the control of capital (on the basis of the sale of labour-power from worker to capitalist), and in the sphere of production, is productive. The strength of this distinction is that it is the only one which can be drawn from the labour theory of value with its vision that the production of value and surplus value is the basis for all economic and other processes in capitalist society. The distinction between the two types of labour is the starting point for understanding the role played by economic agents in capitalist social formations. It should, however, be emphasised that it is only the starting point. To take it as the whole would be to see society only in economic terms. It would, for example, be quite wrong to identify the working class with productive labourers while all others are consigned to the capitalist class or petty bourgeoisie.

These last remarks bring us to the work of Poulantzas (1975), who recognises the significance that the productive/unproductive classification has for the analysis of classes and class struggle. His presentation of the matter demonstrates a careful reading of Marx's classification and he makes clear that classes cannot be analysed in terms of their economic determination alone. But he then argues that only productive labourers are members of the working class (thereby excluding shop assistants, dustmen etc.). Thus we find that whereas, as we have noted elsewhere (Fine and Harris (1976a)), Poulantzas generally over-emphasises political relations, here he swings to the opposite pole, over-emphasis on economic determination.

We have stated that Marx's approach is easy to understand. Nevertheless the neo-Ricardian and Fundamentalist approaches fail to follow Marx's and it is easy to see why. In volume I of *Capital* Marx perceived 'that the production of surplus value has at all times been made, by classical political economists, the distinguishing characteristic of the productive labourer. Hence, their definition of a productive labourer changes with their comprehension of surplus value. Thus the Physiocrats insist that only agricultural labour is productive, since . . . with them, surplus value has no existence except in the form of rent.' (p. 509). The Fundamentalists insist with some inconsistencies that only labour whose products can be accumulated is productive since with them, surplus value has no existence except in the form of accumulation. The neo-Ricardians insist that all labour that is exploited is productive since with them, surplus value has no existence except in the form of surplus product. Marx himself insists that only industrial labour is productive, since with him surplus value has no existence apart from production under capital.

Marx's categorisation, although developed before the significance of state employees and of education and health care had reached present proportions, is applicable to today's problems. As we have indicated elsewhere (Fine and Harris (1976*b*)) it is the basis for studying the fact that in times of crisis the capitalist state cuts expenditure on welfare services. But as we shall see in Chapter 8 when we discuss state monopoly capitalism, the dynamic of state expenditure can only be fully grasped by an analysis of class struggle, in which the productive/unproductive distinction is only one element.

4
The Law of the Tendency of the Rate of Profit to Fall

4.1 Composition of Capital

In the previous chapter we have explained the significance of the debate over the transformation problem and the productive/unproductive labour distinction. Quite apart from the question of whether the positions taken are faithful to 'what Marx actually said' we have demonstrated the strengths and weaknesses of the different contributions in their ability to develop an understanding of capitalist economic life as a whole on the basis of its hidden, inner characteristics. But the force of the arguments over these questions is best appreciated by examining them together with debates over the economic laws of development of capitalism.

One debate on laws of motion has been central to much of British Marxist economics. It concerns the law of the tendency of the rate of profit to fall (TRPF). It is generally agreed that Marx in *Capital* and the *Grundrisse* put forward as a law of capitalism that the rate of profit has a tendency to fall: the laws of production and accumulation 'produce for the social capital a growing absolute mass of profit, and a falling rate of profit'. No one disputes that Marx considered this law to be of fundamental significance: it is 'in every respect the most fundamental law of modern economy, and the most important for understanding the most difficult relations. It is the most important law from the historical stand-point.' Beyond this there is no agreement. In order to appraise the neo-Ricardian and Fundamentalist interpretations of the law we begin by stating our own interpretation (in this and the next section).

58

Discussion of the law has necessarily employed the concept of the composition of capital, because for Marx 'a continuously rising organic composition of capital . . . is represented by a falling general rate of proift', *Capital*, vol. III, p. 213. There has been relatively little controversy over the concept of the composition of capital. Rather it has been seen more as an algebraic convenience (or inconvenience) in defining the rate of profit. However, a clear statement of the distinctions between three concepts of the composition of capital is essential for understanding Marx's law of TRPF, although as we shall see this is not usually appreciated. The concepts employed by Marx are those of the technical composition, the value composition and the organic composition. The technical composition (TCC) is the ratio of the mass of means of production consumed per production period (i.e. abstracting from fixed capital) to the mass of wage goods. It is a ratio of physical, material, quantities and hence unmeasurable by a single index. The value composition (VCC) is an expression for the same ratio measured in terms of the current values of means of production and wage goods consumed. It is therefore the ratio of constant to variable capital, C/V. Now for the organic composition (OCC). Since this is usually expressed by the same ratio C/V (although see Sections 4.3 and 4.4 for a different expression), the reader may wonder in what sense the OCC differs from the VCC. The point is that the technical composition is, for Marx, always increasing as accumulation and more productive techniques are employed. This increase in productivity changes the values per unit of means of production and wage goods; it reduces them and may do so at differential rates. Whereas the VCC is based on these always changing values, the OCC abstracts from these changes. It is C/V where the elements of the means of production and wage goods are valued at their 'old values.' Therefore, changes in the OCC are directly proportional to changes in the technical composition whereas changes in the VCC are not. The distinction can be treated as that between two index numbers, as does Steedman (1977), but in fact it is not a purely quantitative matter for it profoundly affects the interpretation of the law of TRPF.

To emphasise the distinction, let us examine Marx's definitions. He states that the value composition, VCC, is 'determined by the proportion in which it [capital] is divided into constant capital . . . or variable capital.' On the other hand 'I call the value composition in so far as it is determined by its technical composition and mirrors the changes of the latter, the *organic composition* of capital, [OCC]. Whenever I refer to the composition of capital without further qualification, its organic composition is always understood.' (vol. I, p. 612). Marx is clearly making a distinction between the VCC and the OCC, and the basis of this distinction is an understanding of the composition of capital 'in a two fold sense', 'on the side of value' and 'on the side of material' (vol. I, p. 612). Marx is separating two dialectically related processes: first, the increasing OCC associated with the rising TCC and productivity increase described earlier, and second, the consequent reduction in the values of commodities associated with that productivity increase. The overall effect of the two processes on the composition of capital, the technical and value changes, is captured by the VCC. To repeat, the OCC mirrors the TCC while the 'altered value-composition of the capital, however, only shows approximately the change in the composition of its material constituents' (vol. I p. 623).

The quotations from *Capital*, vol. I where the distinction is most forcibly expressed were added to later editions of the work as clarifications. They do, however, precisely correspond to the concepts which Marx employed earlier while writing *Theories of Surplus Value*, Part III. The clearest statement there is 'the organic composition of capital. By this we mean the technological composition' (*TSV*, III, p. 382) and the distinction between this and the VCC which differs from the TCC is then elaborated. It is clear, therefore, that at the time Marx wrote on the law of TRPF, using the concept of organic composition, he had already distinguished it from the value composition; the former being based on 'old values', the latter on 'new values'.

Failure to appreciate this distinction reflects a failure to understand the complex unity of production, exchange and distribution. For the distinction between old and new values, between the OCC and the VCC, is based on the unity between the spheres of production and exchange. The new levels of productivity are created in the sphere of production, but only become established as new values through the exchange of the commodities concerned. Thus the VCC is only formed on the basis of the complex articulation of production, exchange and distribution. The OCC, however, exists at a higher level of abstraction; it exists within the sphere of production abstracting from exchange and distribution (although as we have explained in Chapter 1 abstraction does not mean ignoring or assuming away the other spheres). Here the distinction between 'old' and 'new' values is not based on a chronological but on a conceptual distinction, for both the OCC and VCC are always and simultaneously subject to variation. Consequently the debate between Glyn (1972), (1973) and Murray (1973) over whether the OCC should be evaluated at current or historical values is essentially irrelevant to the distinction necessary for an understanding of the law of the TRPF.

We can now employ these concepts of the composition of capital to analyse the law of TRPF.

4.2   The Tendency of the Rate of Profit to Fall

In the chapter on *The Law as Such* in *Capital*, vol. III, Marx considers the value rate of profit:

$$r = S/C + V = (S/V)/(C/V) + 1 = \text{ rate of exploitation/value composition} + 1$$

and argues that if C/V rises and S/V does not rise sufficiently, the rate of profit will fall. For Marx, however, it appears in places that there is no 'if': the law of TRPF appears as an inevitable aspect of accumulation. Our view is that this law is an inevitable concomitant of accumulation but the law must be understood as the law of the *tendency* of the rate of profit to fall; it is not a law which predicts actual falls in the rate of profit (in value or price terms). To clarify this, we must consider the structure of Marx's argument in terms of the different levels of abstraction which are employed in the three chapters (13 to 15) of *Capital* vol. III, Part III entitled 'The Law as Such', 'Counteracting Influences' and 'Exposition of the Internal Contradictions of the Law'.

In the third of these chapters Marx is concerned with the effects on the surface of society of the law of TRPF, the counteracting influences and the contradictions between these. These effects take the form of 'over-production, speculation, crises, and surplus-capital alongside surplus-population'. These are not simple effects of the law of TRPF or of the counteracting influences, but of both of these existing in a complex contradictory unity: 'From time to time the conflict of antagonistic agencies finds vent in crises. The crises are always but momentary and forcible solutions of the existing contradictions.

The concept of crises is, therefore, at a lower level of abstraction than the concepts involved in the law of TRPF and the counteracting influences: it is constructed on the basis of them. Consider the law as such. It is constructed by abstracting from all distributional changes and from all changes in values except for those which immediately and directly result from changes in the TCC. In short, Marx specifies the law as the consequence of a rising OCC. His method in deducing the law is therefore to abstract from the *indirect* effects of the rising technical composition of capital, to abstract from changes in the rate of exploitation and, since we are dealing with the value rate of profit, to abstract from the effects of price and wage changes on the rate of profit. With these abstractions it follows tautologically that the rate of profit in value terms falls. The significance of this proposition can only be seen when it is considered together with the counteracting influences and the complex effects which are produced. But even at the present stage it would be wrong to dismiss the law as a 'mere' tautology for it can already be seen that it is constructed on the basis of the concepts which come before it in *Capital*. It is the direct effect of the rising technical composition of capital; and the necessity of that tendency itself follows from Marx's analysis of capital as self-expanding value, an analysis constructed from the concepts of the commodities, money, labour, and value.

The law as such then is constructed by abstracting from many complications. The counteracting influences begin to take account of these complications. Marx's presentation of the counteracting influences appears to be a rather arbitrarily delimited list of factors with analysis of the way in which each operates. The list is the same as that proposed by J. S. Mill and Marx prefaces it by the warning that 'the following are the most general counter-balancing forces' only. Those enumerated are chiefly concerned with the distributional effects which can only be understood in terms of the articulation of production, exchange, and distribution. Under this heading are to be considered increasing intensity of exploitation, depression of wages, foreign trade, increase in joint-stock capital, and relative over-population (which encourages low wages). As a result of these factors the effect on the rate of profit of increases in the composition of social capital will be counteracted through changes in distribution between labour and capital.

In addition, Marx includes the cheapening of the elements of constant and variable capital. These counteracting tendencies (which reduce the value of capital advanced and increase the rate of surplus value) are to be associated with the formation of the VCC and the distributional struggle between capital and labour over the value of wages respectively, whereas the law as such is associated with the rising OCC. Distributional struggle over the value of labour-power is the direct product of capital's need, through accumulation, for an expanded and centralised labour-force. The changes wrought in the OCC and VCC are also direct products of the accumulation of capital.

Thus in considering the counteracting influences, Marx introduces accumulation's effects on distribution and on the value composition of capital. They are at the same level of abstraction as the law as such in the sense that the counteracting influences are not predicated upon the concept of the law – they are not the effects or results of the tendency of the rate of profit to fall. Instead, both the law of TRPF and the counteracting influences are equally the effect of capitalist accumulation with its necessary concomitant of a rising technical composition (reflected in Marx's analysis by a rising organic composition but a value composition which does not necessarily rise). As Marx puts it, 'the *same* influences which produce a tendency in the general rate of profit to fall, *also* call forth counter-effects' (emphasis added). In the light of this we think that the name 'law of the TRPF' is something of a misnomer. The law in its broad definition is in fact 'the law of the tendency of the rate of profit to fall and its counteracting influences'.

Our interpretation of Marx's law has several implications which are worth elaborating before we critically appraise other interpretations. First, it is advisable to clarify some semantic issues. When Marx refers to an economic law he explicitly means a tendency. He makes this clear in the very title of vol. III, chapter 13, and the first paragraph of chapter 14; and elsewhere (for example *Capital* vol. III, p. 175) he states that it is the meaning of all economic laws. But the meaning of a tendency is understood differently by different writers. One meaning in the present context is that if one collects data on the rate of profit over a definite period of history one will observe a definite downward trend (or regression line). We shall call this an 'empirical tendency'. A second meaning is that if one abstracts from the counteracting influences one identifies an 'underlying' direction of movement of the rate of profit. This interprets a tendency as a proposition developed at a certain level of abstraction which by itself yields no general predictions about actual movements in the rate of profit. Actual movements depend on a complicated relationship between the tendency and the counteracting influences which have been abstracted from – their particular balance at particular times. We shall call this an 'abstract tendency'. The latter is Marx's concept of the law of the TRPF. The observable effect of the law cannot be a simple tendency for the actual rate of profit (in value or price terms) to fall. The effects of the law (which, being constructed from the law as broadly defined are at a lower level of abstraction) must be the effects of the complex contradictions between the tendency of the rate of profit to fall and the conteracting influences. One such effect is crises which are necessary at times to temporarily resolve the contradictions, another may in fact be actual falls in the rate of profit. But if the latter effect occurs it cannot be understood as a simple manifestation of the law. It is a manifestation of the complex internal contradictions of the law. Hence the title of Marx's chapter 15 where he considers the law of TRPF *and* counteracting influences is 'Exposition of the *Internal* Contradictions of the Law' (emphasis added). What has been shown is that these internal contradictions involve an analysis of the complex articulation of production, exchange, and distribution.

But if the significance of the law of the TRPF is that it is an abstract tendency that co-exists with the abstract tendency for the counteracting influences to operate, why then did Marx in Chapter 13 write of the law of the tendency of the rate of profit to fall and only subsequently bring the counter-acting influences into the discussion of the law and its effects? Is it simply an *accident* of the order of exposition? We consider it follows from the *logical* order of exposition. For, while the counteracting influences, and the tendency itself are simultaneous (albeit contradictory) products of accumulation, the tendency (associated with the rising OCC) can be studied in abstraction from circulation and the distribution of surplus value. On the other hand, the study of the counteracting influences (associated with the formation of the VCC for which the effects of the rising OCC and the reduction of the value of constant and variable capital are integrated) presupposes the formation of new values and a new rate of surplus value through the integration of production with exchange relations. Indeed, it is through exchange that the internal contradictions between the tendencies are expressed. Consequently the TRPF can only appear through its effects derived from its articulation with the counteracting influences, and these in turn can only be examined in relation to the TRPF. In short, the law of the TRPF is an abstract and not an empirical tendency.

4.3 Neo-Ricardian Interpretations of the Law

Having set out our interpretation of the law of TRPF we are now in a position to consider the neo-Ricardian interpretation and critique of the law. That position is best represented in the writings of Steedman (1972), Hodgson (1974) and Himmelweit (1974). Many of the points they develop were already known in less developed form before the recent debates and had been summarised by Meek (1967) and Sweezy (1949). Essential to the critiques is the failure to distinguish between the OCC and the VCC. The two are treated as synonymous, but this conceals the relationship between production, distribution and exchange that is implicit in the distinction between the two concepts. In effect, neo-Ricardians assume that increases in productivity and the formation of new values are automatically and simultaneously achieved. As a result, like us in a sense, they treat the tendency and the counteracting tendencies as having equal status; but, unlike us, the effects of these tendencies are seen as being united by simply adding together the resulting changes brought about on the (price) rate of profit. They do not see the tendency and counteracting tendencies as existing in a contradictory unity.

In essence then, neo-Ricardians are concerned to investigate the validity of the law in terms of whether the simple sum of the effects of the tendency and counteracting tendencies do or do not lead to a fall in the (price) rate of profit. This inevitably leads to a 'logical proof' of the invalidity of the law of TRPF (or, at least, their interpretation of it) by demonstrating that a rising TCC does not necessarily involve a rising value composition (or, as they call it 'organic composition' – the two are essentially indistinguishable for them); that if the VCC does rise this does not necessarily cause falls in the rate of profit for the real source of falls in the rate of profit can only be wage increases, the result of class struggle over distribution in the sphere of exchange. (Since the models are generally constructed in terms of prices rather than values, wage increases are the analogue of falls in the rate of exploitation.)

The first point in the neo-Ricardian argument is that the value (organic) composition is an irrelevant concept (Hodgson, Steedman), just as value itself is. It should be replaced by the concept of dated labour and this view inevitably follows from their concentration on a price of production model (for a critique of which see Chapter 2). In such a model embodied labour is treated simply as a cost and prices are the sum of these costs each multiplied by a factor which depends upon the rate of profit and the date at which the labour was expended. By way of analogy, labour costs are treated very much like loans: the longer ago they were incurred the greater the profit that has to be included in their selling price. For neo-Ricardians then, there is no qualitative difference between dead and living labour as such. There is only the quantitative difference that labour expended in the current period bears either zero or one period's profit mark-up whereas labour expended in previous periods on producing means of production bears a profit mark-up compounded according to the number of periods that have elapsed. For Marx, however, eschewing the dated labour concept of means of production, the qualitative distinction between dead and living labour – the fact that means of production are dead labour whenever it was expended – is all-important. It is captured in the concept of value composition. This concept emphasises the distinction between constant capital (dead labour) which does not create value, and variable capital which is the source of living labour and which does create value. It is no accident that the importance of this distinction escapes the neo-Ricardians. For what it represents is the relationship in aggregate between capital and labour as classes in the sphere of production, whereas as we saw in Chapter 2 the neo-Ricardians' interest in class relations is at a level where the antagonism between the two great classes in production is obscured by competition between and within classes in exchange and distribution.

The second neo-Ricardian argument is that even if we accept the concept of the value ('organic') composition, a rise in the technical composition of capital does not necessarily imply a rise in 'organic' composition (Hodgson). The rise in technical composition, since it raises the productivity of labour, will lower the values of commodities: more commodities can be produced in a given number of labour hours. Assuming that the values of means of production fall in this process, then, depending on the rate of fall, the increasing mass of means of production may not involve an increasing value. The value of constant capital may rise, fall or stay unchanged, and therefore the value composition may not rise even though the technical composition of capital has risen.

A third strand in the neo-Ricardian critique is the idea that, even if the organic composition does increase, the rate of profit will not necessarily fall. It is a proposition put forward in different ways by Hodgson (1974) and Himmelweit (1974). Hodgson's argument for this proposition is extremely weak since it reasons by a false analogy between neo-classical economics and Marx's theory.

Himmelweit's argument is more worthy of consideration. She argues in a model expressed in terms of prices of production rather than values and she adopts $c'/v'+s'$ rather than c'/v' as the measure of organic composition (where the dashes denote price rather than value quantification). Within a neo-Ricardian model of prices of production it can be shown that, given the state of technology, there is a unique inverse relationship between wages and the rate of profit: if wages go up, the rate of profit must go down and vice versa. Indeed this is one of Sraffa's (1960) most significant results for neo-Ricardianism. Himmelweit argues from this that a rise in the wage rate is the sole cause of a fall in the rate of profit given the state of technology. Further, a rise in the wage rate, inducing individual capitalists to change to new but previously available techniques to offset the rise in wages, *brings about* in aggregate a higher 'organic' composition and level of productivity. This rise in productivity actually *stems* the fall in the rate of profit which is being caused by rising wage rates. Therefore to the extent that the 'organic' composition rises, this represents on the one hand a response to rising wages, and on the other, a slowing of the tendency of the rate of profit to fall. Far from the rising 'OCC' being associated with the law of the TRPF, it is to be associated with the counteracting influences! The capitalist class as a whole benefits from the fact that the new techniques, introduced by individual capitalists for their own gain, reduce the effects of rising wages, whereas Marx argues that the competitive actions of individual capitalists in introducing new techniques (raising TCC) are at the basis of the falling rate of profit and therefore tendentially harm the class as a whole.

The contrast between Himmelweit's conclusions and Marx's arises because the structure and status of each and every concept differs between the two writers. For Himmelweit a distribution phenomenon, the movement of the wage rate, is primary and the motive force (and this phenomenon is considered only as an exchange phenomenon). Why the wage rate should rise remains unexplained, although for neo-Ricardians it is usually based on the outcome of class struggle as the proletariat is strengthened by the rise in employment brought about by accumulation. However, this accumulation is itself unexplained, imposed externally upon the theory. Indeed in neo-Ricardian theory there is precisely no motive for capital accumulation, because it is assumed that production can be undertaken at any and every scale. Although there can be some rather hair-splitting debate about whether Sraffa (1960) assumes constant returns to scale, this assumption is now generally employed in neo-Ricardian theory. Therefore, no economies (or diseconomies) of scale are to be reaped by accumulation and the motive for accumulation is untheorised.

In contrast, for Marx, accumulation of capital is the primary and motive force, from which the movements of wage rates (and other categories) are derivative: 'the rate of accumulation is the independent not the dependent variable; the rate of wages the dependent, not the independent variable'. Nor is this accumulation imposed in a vacuum. It follows from the coercive force of competition.

From this it can be seen that the two differ over the concept of competition. For Himmelweit as a neo-Ricardian, competition exists only in three senses: to equalise the rates of profit between capitalists (and wages between workers), in distributional struggle between capital and labour over the level of wages, and as the stimulus to cost reduction. The last causes capitalists to change their choice of technique (from a given set) when the wage-rate changes. In contrast, for Marx, competition exists first and foremost as a stimulus to accumulation and expansion of production. The organic composition and productivity rise even without the prior stimulus of rising wages. When this happens, then even in Himmelweit's price of production model, the rate of profit will fall to the extent that wages rise. And in Marx's approach developed at that level of abstraction where the value of labour-power is constant wages *will* rise, since to maintain equality between wages and a constant value of labour-power, wages must rise as labour productivity rises. For the rise in labour productivity means that the value embodied in each wage commodity falls;

if the value of labour-power is to be constant and equal to wages, then wages must rise to allow more commodities, and hence an equal amount of total value, to be received by workers. The extent to which wages do in fact maintain their value will depend upon the strength of capital and labour in distributional struggle as well as the extent to which the value of wage-goods is reduced. But these factors, as elements of the counteracting tendencies, cannot be seen, when analysing their effects, in isolation from their contradictory unity with the development of production as expressed in the law of the TRPF. This analysis demonstrates the significance of value analysis since Himmelweit's concentration on price of production and wage-rates diverts attention from the question of the value of labour-power. More than that, it actually prevents an analysis which takes into account the articulation of the spheres of production, exchange and distribution with production as fundamental, for, as we have shown in Chapter 2 this articulation cannot be understood without value theory. Thus Himmelweit is forced to consider matters from the one-sided exchange-based view of distribution.

What then is the conclusion of the neo-Ricardian critique of the law of the TRPF. Hodgson and Himmelweit both argue that the element of truth in Marx's law is that a rise in the value composition (numerically equated to $C/S+V$) if it occurs, will involve a fall in the maximum attainable rate of profit – in the rate of profit that would be obtained if wages were zero. This is because when wages are zero (i.e. $V=O$) the reciprocal of the 'organic' composition $S+V/C$ is identical to the rate of profit $S/C+V$ since both are then equal to S/C where S now represents the total working day. The important point for neo-Ricardianism, however, is that the rate of profit is below its maximum since wages are greater than zero. As Himmelweit concludes, the fact that the maximum rate of profit will fall if the 'organic' composition rises says nothing about whether there is a tendency for the actual rate of profit to fall. What is emphasised is that changes in wage-rates are the sources of changes in the profit rate. Class struggle over distribution in the sphere of exchange is for them everything (see Bhaduri (1969)). This is the theoretical basis for the empirical work of Glyn and Sutcliffe (1972) which we discuss below in Chapter 5.

Finally it must be made clear that an almost automatic consequence of the neo-Ricardian treatment of the law is to view it as an empirical law, predicting actual falls in the observable (price) rate of profit and rises in the value composition of capital (see in particular Hodgson (1974)). This has given rise to a number of direct attempts to interpret and confirm or refute the law empirically (Gillman (1957), Mandel (1975), Hodgson (1974)). In general, these contributions take the law to refer to the secular development of capitalism, while the law in fact refers to the cycle of production. Even so cyclical movements in the rate of profit and composition of capital cannot be explained or predicted simply by the law. But if Marx was not predicting an empirical tendency, if the rate of profit in value or price terms may go up, down or neither over any particular time period, why say that its movements are subject to a law? At one level we have given an answer – the law refers to an abstract tendency not an empirical tendency. The substantive problem posed by Hodgson (1977), for example, is what is the significance of a law if it does not offer simple predictions of an empirical trend? The point which the question fails to grasp is that an abstract tendency *does* have a connection with observable phenomena even though it does not involve simple predictions of trends. The TRPF and tendency for counteracting influences to operate actually exist in capitalism in a contradictory relationship with each other. The existence of these contradictions gives rise to crises, booms, and the associated cycles of production and exchange. These, with their rhythm of unemployment, concentration and centralisation and other phenomena are the observable 'predictions' of Marx's abstract tendency. Indeed, particular movements in the actual observable rate of profit are associated with these cycles. At times the rate of profit will actually fall, at others it will actually rise. These movements are not arbitrary but are based on the abstract tendencies and their contradictions. Thus we would expect that crises which result from these contradictions give rise (through the restructuring of capital and other forces which they generate) to an increase in the rate of profit as the basis for a cyclical upturn. The point is simply that these definite movements in observable phenomena are the complex ultimate result of contradictions between abstract tendencies; they are not the simple empirical tendency of falls in the rate of profit which only writers such as Hodgson would endow with the title 'law'. It is this belief that the only significant theoretical propositions are those which consist of simple predictions of observable phenomena (rather than those which see such phenomena as resulting from contradictory complex relationships) which entitles us to argue that neo-Ricardians tend to employ an empiricist methodology despite protestations to the contrary.

4.4   Fundamentalist Interpretations of the Law

At the opposite extreme the Fundamentalist interpretation (Yaffe (1972) and Cogoy (1973)) emphasises the immanent contradictions of capital as the basis of the law of TRPF. These are seen as being located within the sphere of production and associated with capital-in-general rather than with competition.

Yaffe considers the problem in two stages. First he argues that accumulation necessarily involves a rise in the technical *and* value composition of capital and, second, he argues that this rise is not offset by increases in the rate of exploitation, since there are definite limits to its rate of increase. Therefore, he concludes, there is a tendency for the value rate of profit to fall. The substance of his argument concerns the rising value composition (which he mistakenly calls the OCC); the inevitability of this tendency, he argues, stems from the very nature of capital. The concept of capital implies a contradiction since capital is 'value in process'; it is self-expanding value which necessarily strives for expansion without limit, but its self-expansion is based on the labour of the working class and this is necessarily a limited basis since the population and length of the working day cannot be expanded without limit. As the resolution of this contradiction, capital therefore must make itself as independent as possible from its limited base by increasing the technical composition of capital; employing, that is, a greater proportion of machinery and raising labour productivity so that a greater amount of raw materials is worked up with a given amount of living labour. Furthermore, this must involve an increase in the value composition, the relative value of constant and variable capital employed.

The last step is particularly contentious. Why must a rise in TCC be associated with a rise in value composition? Since the latter is calculated at 'new values' it may fall while the TCC rises, as the neo-Ricardians never tire of emphasising and as Marx himself makes clear. Yaffe attempts to rescue the theory that the value and technical compositions are necessarily correlated by appealing to Marx's rule for installing new machinery. But the argument is invalid (and its internal inconsistency has been noted by Catephores (1973)). Yaffe is therefore left with a mere assertion that the value composition (his 'organic composition') rises and the rate of profit falls.

The problem is that Yaffe has confused the value and organic compositions. In the terms set out in Sections 4.1 and 4.2 the truth is that when the TCC rises the OCC must rise, but what happens to the value composition depends on the counteracting influences. In terms of the true meanings of VCC and OCC Yaffe's argument can be framed as follows. As TCC rises, OCC rises and this produces a tendency for the rate of profit to fall. Thus the tendency is based in the sphere of production. So far the argument is valid. But then Yaffe has to take the further steps of arguing that the counteracting influences are at a lower level of abstraction and that the law as such always dominates the counteracting influences so that the rising organic composition is expressed in a rising value composition. This is wrong in Marx's terms since it fails to grasp the complex unity of the law as such and the counteracting influences, each with equal status. Moreover the second of these steps can only be founded on assertions. The assertions are made with great force by Yaffe because he, like the neo-Ricardians, sees the law of TRPF as an empirical law, a statement that the rate of profit will be negatively correlated with the TCC as in a downward-sloping regression line.

Similar faults are found in Cogoy's (1973) contribution. He builds a 'model' in which, unusually, the OCC is defined as $C/S+V$ and this is distinguished from the VCC (defined C/V). The purpose of this definition of the OCC is to eliminate changes in the rate of exploitation (value of labour-power).

On this basis Cogoy claims to be concentrating on the sphere of production, for distributional struggle is thereby abstracted from. Thus Cogoy is instinctively right to associate the OCC with production in abstraction but, in comparison to the distinction drawn in Section 4.1, he has incorrectly drawn the distinction between OCC and VCC.

The use of living labour, $S+V$ (the length of the working day), as opposed to variable capital V to measure the organic composition has the effect of capturing changes in the value of constant capital while ignoring changes in the value of variable capital. In contrast to the law as stated in Sections 4.1, 4.2, constant capital is measured by Cogoy at 'new values' which are achieved automatically, while variable capital is measured at 'old values'. Although this maintains the distinction between dead and living labour, it does so in an arbitrary fashion, especially when it is borne in mind that reductions in the value of constant capital reduce, *ceteris paribus*, the value of labour-power to the extent that the value of wage goods embodies the value of physical means of production. In addition, there are further problems with Cogoy's statement. Abstracting from distributional struggle in his way is equivalent to examining movements in the maximum rate of profit. As the neo-Ricardians have shown, this falls *if* the OCC, defined as $C/S+V$, rises. Cogoy has to assume that it does rise, and this he does by arbitrarily assuming that constant capital always grows faster than the mass of living labour. This is inconsistent because more surplus value becomes accumulated than is being produced. Leaving this aside, the end result is identical to the neo-Ricardian conclusion – that the *maximum* rate of profit falls if the ratio of constant capital to living labour rises. The only difference is that for Cogoy this ratio *must* rise and that changes in the maximum as opposed to the actual rate of profit are fundamental because they abstract from distributional struggle.

To sum up, neo-Ricardianism's thrust is that the idea of a rising organic composition cannot be the basis of the law of TRPF and that, instead, we should focus on changes in the rate of exploitation in price terms, changes brought about by class struggle over wages, as the source of a falling rate of profit. In contrast, the Fundamentalists argue that the law of

TRPF stems from a rising organic composition and that the latter is inherent in the nature of capital. Both schools, however, suffer from the same weakness – a misinterpretation of Marx's method and the meaning of the law.

Neo-Ricardians and Fundamentalists alike consider the law to predict falls in the actual (value or price) rate of profit, falls which are the simple effect of a rising technical composition. Neo-Ricardians seek to disprove such a proposition by, among other things, emphasising the role of two groups of Marx's counteracting influences: the cheapening of the elements of constant capital which may prevent the value composition rising with the technical composition, and changes in distribution related to wage struggles. Fundamentalists recognise the existence of counteracting influences but treat them as secondary, transient factors so that the effects of the law of TRPF continually reappear as actual falls preceding crises. The neo-Ricardian position is the reverse and is summarised by Hodgson's view (1974) that the counteracting influences may be considered as the law and the tendency of the rate of profit to fall as contingent. Both schools consider that what is a law and what a 'mere' influence is an empirical matter, a question of the frequency with which one is manifested rather than the other.

The burden of our own interpretation is that the existence of both the tendency of the rate of profit to fall and of counteracting influences has the status of a law in the sense that both are inevitable products of capitalist accumulation. One cannot preface the counteracting influences with the adjective 'mere'. The distinction between the law of TRPF and the counteracting influences is not one of their relative empirical or logical significance. It is a distinction based solely on the fact that Marx isolates and considers separately the different effects of accumulation; the concept of organic composition is employed to analyse the former and the concept of value composition to analyse the latter. The importance of the distinction between these two concepts has escaped neo-Ricardian and Fundamentalist writers. This has profound effects on their interpretations of crises, to which we now turn.

5
Theory of Crisis

5.1 Partial Theories of Crises' Forms and Causes

For Marx accumulation is the essence of capitalism: 'Accumulate, accumulate: that is Moses and the prophets.' But capitalist accumulation necessarily follows a cyclic path which is dominated by the crisis phase. The study of cyclical accumulation is a twofold venture: it is the study of the cause of crises and of their forms. Existing theories of crises frequently confuse the forms of crises with the causes and this generally arises because they concentrate on one of the phenomena of crises to the exclusion of others. Before turning to these, two things must be emphasised. First, the crises with which we are concerned are economic crises rather than general social crises; they are identified by a violent interruption in the circuits of capital. Second, since in the Marxist concept capitalist accumulation is necessarily punctuated by crises, the theory of the cause of crises must demonstrate that none is accidental but all arise from a common foundation which is inherent in capitalism.

There are three main theories of crises supported by Marxists, although these theories are rarely stated in abstract form but are found embedded in concrete analyses. As well as neo-Ricardian and Fundamentalist theories of crises, underconsumption theories are put forward by some who claim to follow Marx. None of these schools in fact comprises Marx's theory of crises.

The neo-Ricardian position on crises is best summarised by Glyn and Sutcliffe (1972) in their analysis of the post-war

76

British economy. Surprisingly, since we have seen that neo-Ricardians reject Marx's law of the tendency of the rate of profit to fall, these authors argue that crises result from falls in the rate of profit. The paradox disappears when it is realised that they are talking about the rate of profit calculated at market prices rather than at values (or prices of production). Thus the cause of the fall in the rate of profit is seen as the result of a rise in wages at the expense of profits and this itself is the result of workers' relative strength in class struggle. This balance of forces is not explained on any general basis but only as the effect of a specific conjuncture. And the class struggle to which it relates is of a partial nature; it is conflict over distribution in the sphere of exchange (wage-rates).

These features of Glyn and Sutcliffe's theory are characteristic of the neo-Ricardian emphasis on class conflict over distribution as the dominant contradiction of capitalism. But that school's theory of crisis does not always restrict the protagonists to labour and capital within one nation; to analyse the 1970s, crisis writers such as Gordon (1975) broaden the terms to include conflict between labour, capital, the state, and foreign capital. (Glyn and Sutcliffe also include the intensification of international competition in world trade as an explanation of the 'profit squeeze'.) The crucial idea remains that the conflict is over distribution phenomena – wages, profits, taxes, terms of trade. From the point of view of the economy the balance of forces in such struggles at particular conjunctures is purely contingent. This gives neo-Ricardianism both its strength and its weakness: its strength because it indicates that the 'subjective' actions of the working class (even if focused upon distributional struggle) have a determining role to play in capitalism's developments; its weakness because their theory implies that crises are 'accidental' rather than the necessary concomitant of the complex contradictions between the forces and relations of production.

Fundamentalists, on the other hand, locate the source of crises in the law of the TRPF which, as we have explained in the previous chapter, they analyse within the sphere of production in terms of capital-in-general (i.e. attempting to abstract from competition). This position is best represented by Yaffe (1972), but see also Bullock and Yaffe (1975). The law of the TRPF is seen as sometimes being masked by counteracting influences and at other times comes to the surface in the form of an actual decline. When it does make this appearance it induces crises and these crises overcome the contradiction of capital for which the falling rate of profit is merely the form of expression; but in overcoming the contradiction, the barrier to accumulation, the crises remove it to a higher level. Economic crisis is seen as *the* major counteracting influence to the tendency of the rate of profit to fall (although Marx considers it as the resolution of the contradictions of the tendency and the counteracting influences rather than a counteracting influence itself). Yaffe argues that the law of TRPF is located exclusively within the sphere of production, but that crises can only be analysed after competition and activities in the sphere of exchange are introduced. The processes by which the crisis counteracts the falling rate of profit and restores the conditions for accumulation include forces located within the sphere of production (e.g. restructuring of productive capital), those located within the sphere of exchange (e.g. depreciation of the prices of commodities) and distributional phenomena. This analysis of crises is the opposite of the neo-Ricardians'. It emphasises the priority of production rather than exchange and distribution based on exchange, and it locates crises as necessary rather than contingent. In this, Yaffe is closer to advocating Marx's theory of crises whereas neo-Ricardians can only be considered to be rejecting it. However, Yaffe's argument does have its faults and these are related to his treatment of the law of the TRPF. For while he recognises that the course of the crisis is determined by competition (as between capital and labour, as between capitals in the processes of distribution and exchange), his analysis of this is necessarily suspended in isolation from the law of the TRPF which is confined to the sphere of production alone. As a result, the role played by exchange and distribution (and class struggle over them) in economic reproduction must be reduced mechanically to the logical requirements of the laws of production. Otherwise *ad hoc* functions and explanations are assigned to them which cannot be deduced from the logic of production alone (as in Yaffe's Keynesian treatment of state expenditure, on which see Chapter 6).

The misunderstandings about the nature of the law of TRPF which we examined in Chapter 4 have an effect on both Fundamentalist and more eclectic theories of crisis. This is illustrated by Gamble and Walton (1976) and Mandel (1975) respectively. The former, for example, see crises as the simple product of increases in the organic composition of capital (which they confuse with the VCC) and this leads them to interpret all class struggle (including the state's role) in terms of the interest the bourgeoisie supposedly has in restraining the growth of the composition of capital. Mandel (1975), together with Rowthorn (1976), also addresses himself to the question of whether what they call the organic composition has risen, as if this could be the direct cause of crises by its isolated and quantitative effect on the rate of profit.

The third school, underconsumptionism, has a history within Marxism which runs from Rosa Luxemburg (1963) to Baran and Sweezy (1964), although Bleaney (1976) in his careful survey argues that the first does not fit into this school. Its essence is that crises result from a deficiency in the effective demand for commodities for one reason or another. In this it is clearly similar to Keynes's (1936) theory, but the question is whether it is in any sense Marxist. Marx does develop the concept of effective demand and employ it in a remarkable anticipation of Keynes's multiplier analysis of the developments which occur within crises. But these concepts pertain to the form which crises take rather than to their underlying cause. The underconsumptionists, by contrast, take the deficiency of demand as the cause of crises and thereby confuse the form of crises with their cause. Although underconsumptionism is a distinct school of thought some writers, of whom Kalecki (1943) is a leading example, combine it with neo-Ricardian ideas. In such cases the source of underconsumption is seen as the depression of wage rates which reduces workers' effective demand, but the crisis cannot be cured by a rise in wage rates (or employment) for this would reduce the rate of profit (and workers' discipline as jobs become easily obtained).

If underconsumptionism confuses the form of crises with

their cause it is because crises under capitalism do take the form of being precipitated by a failure of demand (unsold goods) whereas in pre-capitalist modes crises took the entirely different form of natural or social upheavals precipitating falls in supply (such as harvest failure). The idea of a failure of demand is that of a break in the circuit of aggregate capital in the phase $C'-M'$. How this form is itself a summary of breaks in the circuits of individual capitals is explored by Itoh (1975), Ergas and Fishman (1975) and Fine (1975*a*). These writers make clear that breaks in the complex articulation of individual circuits, especially through monetary exchange, are the basic form of crises. The individual circuits become desynchronised. But what is demonstrated thereby is only the possibility of crises; the analysis as such says nothing of the cause of crises (although Itoh supplements his analysis with a neo-Ricardian view of causes); by demonstrating only the possibility of crisis, one equally demonstrates the possibility of a crisis-free accumulation in which circuits of capital are not broken despite their anarchic integration through market relations.

5.2   Crises and their Determining Contradictions

The crisis theories examined above are unsatisfactory in several ways but most basically because they are partial as compared with Marx's. Neo-Ricardianism and underconsumption theories see the source of crises in the sphere of exchange; Fundamentalism is unable to see the articulation betwen production, on which it concentrates, and exchange and distribution. But Marx's own theory of crisis is not presented in *Capital* in an easily accessible form. In this section, therefore, we bring its elements together.

Crises, the dominant phase of the cycle, are forcible changes in the progress of capitalist accumulation; not only in the pace of accumulation but also in its internal structure. Marx sees them as necessary in the sense that they forcibly resolve the internal contradictions of accumulation which would otherwise persist. In separate places he describes these contradictions in two apparently separate ways. On one hand Marx sees crises as resolving the contradictions between the spheres of production, exchange and distribution, the tensions and displacements between them. The reader can gain a concrete picture of one such displacement by thinking of the speculative boom which generally precedes crises; there exchange is over-developed in relation to production. On the other hand Marx sees crises as resolving the contradictions between the law of TRPF and the counteracting tendencies. In fact these two formulations are complementary rather than separate for we have already seen (Chapter 4) that the law of TRPF concerns the effect of accumulation within the sphere of production in abstraction whereas the counteracting influences concern the effects within all three spheres. These two formulations of the contradictions which crises have to solve are the elements on which Marx's theory is constructed: the idea of displacement between the spheres is the idea of a particular structural relationship while the effects of accumulation (law of TRPF and counteracting influences) are seen as the dynamic force which explains the development of these contradictions over time.

To see the development of crises we have to examine this dynamic force. Within the sphere of production, capitalist accumulation in the expansion phase of the cycle produces continual revolutions in the labour process, in the forces of production. By itself this produces a tendency for the rate of profit to fall. It also leads to the expulsion of living labour from production. These factors, however, do not necessarily cause the expansionary phase to falter: within the whole circuit of capital the counteracting influences may be such as to maintain or even raise the rate of profit and the rate of accumulation may be such that the relative expulsion of living labour does not become absolute. Continued accumulation on this basis can be thought of as the harmonious development of the three spheres. It also defines the idea that the law of TRPF and the counteracting influences are in harmony rather than antagonistic contradiction with each other. This idea, however, is as much an abstract construction as are Marx's reproduction schema: it abstracts from the fact that the antagonistic contradictions of the law and counteracting influences are ever present so that accumulation carries the seed of its own interruption.

But what is the meaning of these contradictions? How are the counteracting influences in conflict with the TRPF in anything other than a quantitative sense (one pushing the rate of profit up with the other pulling it down)? This conflict is defined as the opposite of the harmonious co-existence of the law and the counteracting influences; it is defined as any conjuncture of the law and the counteracting influences which causes capitalist accumulation to be interrupted. Marx's theory of crisis is the idea that such conjunctures necessarily develop, but they may take several different forms. The simplest is where both the TRPF and the counteracting influences work smoothly but the former is quantitatively more powerful so that the actual rate of profit falls and the stimulus to accumulation thereby disappears. It is wrongly assumed by Fundamentalists that this is the only possible conjuncture which Marx considered to be the basis of crises, and both they and neo-Ricardians consider that accumulation depends upon a positive stimulus to capitalists' motives (the value rate of profit and the price rate of profit respectively). The error of this view can be seen from Marx's emphasis on the mass of surplus value (identified with the mass of profit) as being even more significant than the rate of profit; the ability to accumulate dominates the incentive. In fact, the effect of falls in the rate of profit in producing crises cannot be understood without recognising the significance of the mass of profit or surplus value. For if the rate of profit is seen as a stimulus so that accumulation is positively related to it, its gradual decline should produce a gradual decline in accumulation rather than its sudden interruption. The effect of the *mass* of surplus value in determining the ability to accumulate, however, necessarily involves discontinuities. This is because the ability to accumulate depends not only on the mass of surplus value but also on the minimum size of the mass that can be capitalised. Given the significance of fixed capital and the tendency for the size of fixed capital in each production process to increase, a definite amount of surplus value is required if accumulation is to proceed. If the rate of profit falls but the mass of surplus value remains sufficiently large, accumulation can proceed; if, however, the mass falls below the critical point while retaining a positive increase accumulation must be interrupted.

Falls in the rate of profit and its mass are not the only possible conjunctures characterised by contradiction between TRPF and the counteracting influences. Others arise from the tensions which are involved in the formation of TRPF and the counteracting influences themselves. That is, it is a mistake to picture increases in the organic composition (TRPF) as proceeding smoothly even when accumulation is going ahead; the scrapping of old techniques and the installation of new involve sharp changes rather than gradual trends. Similarly, it is a mistake to picture counteracting influences developing smoothly. Foreign trade, for example, cannot grow in a smooth progression; the international division of labour which it produces involves the development and the closure of whole industries. More significantly, the decline in the value of the elements of constant capital – or, more generally, the formation of the value composition of capital – involves upheavals. For changes in the value composition involve not only the changes in production techniques which underlie the organic composition (TRPF) but also changes in exchange relations. As Marx argues, such changes in values mean that when money-capital comes to be thrown back into the circuit $(M'-C)$ the capitalist finds that the old relations have been transformed (the relative values of $C(LP, MP)$ have altered as have those for $C'-M'$). Therefore the reproduction of capital requires not the reproduction of the old circuit but a leap into a radically new circuit. It requires, that is, a break in the existing circuits, a crisis. Marx describes such a crisis associated with this counteracting influence as: 'This periodical depreciation of existing capital – one of the means immanent in capitalist production to check the fall in the rate of profit . . . disturbs the given conditions, within which the process of circulation and reproduction of capital takes place, and is therefore accompanied by sudden stoppages and crises in the production process.'

The example Marx then gives of this depreciation of capital (*Capital*, vol. III, chapter XV, section III) is one where it follows from an actual fall in the rate of profit; but it is clear that this is only one of the possible conjunctures, for Marx writes that 'these antagonistic agencies counteract each other *simultaneously*' (emphasis added) and the 'different influences may at one time operate predominantly side by side in space and at another succeed each other in time.' (*Capital*, vol. III, p. 249).

In this context, the *devaluation* of capital can be defined in terms of the increasing productivity associated with the increasing OCC, that is with the law of the TRPF. On the other hand, for this devaluation or reduction of values to be expressed and formed through exchange, the capital must be *depreciated*; that is, the VCC formed and the counteracting tendencies realised. In so far as the law of the TRPF and the counteracting tendencies interact smoothly, the devaluation and depreciation of capital are synonymous. But it is over the cycle of production that the two do not act in unison and in recession in particular that capital is depreciated without being devalued, and that the exchange value of capital falls (money appreciates) without a corresponding reduction in values. It is this depreciation on which a renewed accumulation and centralisation can be based, as idle (e.g. bankrupt) capitals are absorbed by those that survive the competitive process.

It seems clear then that Marx sees crises not as the simple effect of actual falls in the rate of profit which are themselves the simple manifestation of the TRPF. They result from the fact that accumulation inevitably causes both the TRPF and the counteracting influences to develop in such a contradictory way that smooth accumulation is impossible. Crises are seen as necessary for the resolution of those contradictions, but in what sense? Marx makes clear that the most fundamental force generated in crises is the scrapping of old techniques and the adoption of more productive ones. This restructuring of capital can temporarily resolve the contradictions which gave rise to crisis whatever their specific appearances. If the rate of profit actually fell, the restructuring of capital would be necessary to restore it (by depreciating but not devaluing the elements of constant and variable capital and increasing the production of relative surplus value) (*Capital*, vol. III, p. 255). If the crisis is precipitated by the depreciation of capital even before a fall in the actual rate of profit has become manifest, this restructuring of capital is itself part of the process of depreciating capital.

5.3   Crises and the Most Complex Phenomena

The preceding section presents Marx's theory of the determining contradictions in crises. These are located in terms of values and are therefore at a relatively high level of abstraction. Remaining at that level, however, prevents us from showing how the observable superficial phenomena associated with crises and the cycle are founded upon these determining contradictions. Let us move on, therefore.

The first task is to complete the picture while remaining at that level of abstraction where values are relevant. For we have not so far introduced money into the analysis. This is easily done. The crisis is the interruption of the circuit of capital so that a part of capital ceases to function as capital. This is true of capital in each of its fundamental forms, productive, commodity *and* money capital. The circulation of money as capital therefore declines or in more familiar language money as the medium of circulation is hoarded. This hoarding is merely the counterpart of a decline in the circulation of commodities and therefore it appears at first to be a rather passive phenomenon in the development of crises. But it has in fact a very active role for the formation of hoards affects money's role as a 'means of payment' (that is, a means for settling debts). Lenders attempt to accumulate hoards by pressing for settlement of debts from those capitals which are in crisis but borrowers default on their debt obligations. This leads to a restriction or even collapse of the credit system which plays an active role in ensuring that the crisis spreads to all capitals from those capitals first affected.

The second task is to examine how market price phenomena, observable wages and profits, are related to the fundamental contradictions we have explored. For this it is necessary to introduce explicitly competition in the sense of the market demand and supply for labour-power (although it should be noted that the adoption of new techniques which we examined in Section 5.2 itself implicitly assumes competition between capitals). The phenomena we have already considered abstract from the fact that the value of wages may diverge from the value of labour-power. Thus we can proceed to analyse how, on the basis of these phenomena, the path of these divergences over the cycle is determined; the abstraction, therefore, is the same as Marx's dictum that wages are the dependent, accumulation the independent variable. Marx's view of the path of wages is straightforward and unexceptionable. It is that the value of wages rises above the value of labour-power as accumulation and economic activity rise, and they fall below it in crises and the ensuing stagnation. The apparent simplicity of this view, however, hides several problems some of which are more easily solved than others. Do these systematic variations in wages themselves have any effect on accumulation? It is clear that they do – for example, depression of wages is one of the counteracting influences and affects the pace of capital's recovery after crisis – but this two-way influence does not lessen the fact that accumulation rather than wages is determinant. Does the value of labour-power itself remain constant over the cycle as is implicitly assumed in Marx's theory? It is reasonable to argue that movements of wages do themselves ultimately affect the value of labour-power (through its moral and historic element). Depression of wages after a crisis can, if sufficiently severe and accompanied by other phenomena (such as ideological attack by the bourgeoisie) push down the value of labour-power; a period of expansion can raise it. This is not inconsistent with Marx's theory of crisis and cycles; in fact, it reinforces it. How does the divergence of wages from the value of labour-power relate to inflation? This is a problem which is inseparable from the role of credit over the cycle and we return to it in Chapter 8, Section 4.

Our next task is to examine the role of class struggle in crises and cycles. The question of the competitive determination of wages, which we have already considered, relates to that of class struggle. Competition over the value of wages is a form of economic class struggle and therefore if we say that the movement of wages is determined by and affects the cycle of accumulation we are saying that this is true of a specific form of class struggle. More general forms of economic class struggle between the proletariat and bourgeoisie are also related to the cycle of accumulation although the particular relationship is specific to each form of struggle. Of these, the most important is struggle over production itself. The process of accumulation involves constant revolutions in the techniques of production, but the pace of these is different at different phases of the cycle. At and immediately after the crisis, for example, the revolution in techniques is dramatic even though (or because) accumulation is zero or low. The proletariat is forced to struggle against this restructuring of capital, against the expulsion of living labour; and this struggle itself has an effect on the duration of the crisis and ensuing slump. Thus, economic class struggle at the level of production is affected by the phases of the cycle but is nevertheless distinct from class struggle over wages (exchange): the strength of the former after a crisis, for example, depends upon the restructuring of capital within the factory in a direct way (e.g. struggle over control of the speed of the production line) whereas the latter depends upon it in an indirect way through its effects upon the reserve army of labour.

Moreover the rhythm of class struggle associated with the cycles of accumulation concerns not only the antagonism between the working class and the bourgeoisie. It also concerns the antagonistic fractions of the bourgeoisie in two major ways. On one hand the relations between interest-bearing and industrial capital (financial and industrial bourgeoisies) change over the cycle. From being harmonious during the phase of expansion they become antagonistic during crises. This is the counterpart at the level of class (fraction) struggle of money ceasing to function as a means of payment and of the accumulation of hoards. Financial capitalists, in particular, attempt to accumulate money in the form of hoards during crises. This may involve a collapse of the credit system. It also involves distributional struggle, since the rise in the interest rate which results from hoarding at time of crisis reduces the portion of total profit which is received by industrial capitalists (profit on enterprise). As Harris (1976) argues, this distributional struggle is determined by the cycle of accumulation rather than being purely accidental; nevertheless it itself has an effect on accumulation.

We can summarise the role of class struggle over the cycle

as follows. The antagonisms which determine the cycle are those located within the sphere of production, which are understood on the basis of values (law of TRPF and counteracting tendencies). There is class struggle on the basis of this antagonism between capital and labour (struggle over the introduction of new techniques, speed of the production line etc.) but crisis is not produced by a simple balance of forces in this struggle. It is not analysable simply as the result of the working class preventing the introduction of new techniques (as bourgeois ideology proclaims); nor simply as the result of capitalists' victory in introducing new techniques (as Fundamentalists might claim). In addition, at a much lower level of abstraction, there is class struggle over market exchange relations, determined by the cycle which results from capitalist production. This struggle concerns market wages primarily, and although it has an effect on the cycle it cannot be taken as determinant as in Glyn and Sutcliffe (1972). Similarly, the struggle over wages in price of production (rather than market) terms cannot be taken as determinant. Finally, the struggle between fractions of the bourgeoisie determined by the cycle has an effect on the cycle.

The cycle and crises are therefore the products of the capital/labour antagonism which manifests itself in production and in exchange and in distribution. Developments at each of these levels involve contradictions and these are related to each other in a hierarchical manner. Crises occur when these contradictions exist in particular relation to each other when, in terms of Althusser's (1969) concept, there is an over-determination of contradictions. Thus, crises are not produced by exchange contradictions (market wages or profits), or by production contradictions (law of TRPF) but by these in a particular relation to each other.

In considering the effect on the cycle of struggle between capitalists and labourers (as classes) care must be taken to understand this struggle as determined by the antagonistic relation of capital and labour. If this is not done class struggle becomes easily misunderstood as the action of classes organised as such and conscious of themselves as classes. It is then a short step to seeing crises as the effect of a capitalist conspiracy (to restructure capital or to push down wages) or of a workers' conspiracy (Luddism or greed). The essence of Marx's analysis, which avoids these failings, is that crises occur through the antagonism of labour and capital (which, although borne by humans, are themselves non-human forces) and that they occur whether or not capitalists and labourers as classes (or individuals) consciously struggle over accumulation.

We have presented here Marx's theory of crises. In doing so we have demonstrated the partial nature of neo-Ricardian and Fundamentalist theories and shown how underconsumptionist theories confuse the form of crises with their cause. But it is commonly asked whether Marx's theory has any relevance for today. After all, Marx's theory takes no account of the role of the state which is now so significant. Nor does it take account to any extent of the rivalry between blocs of capitals organised within a system of national states (inter-imperialist rivalry) and the effect that this has on accumulation. In subsequent chapters, after considering the specificity of modern capitalism we return to the theory of crisis and argue that Marx's theory, far from being outdated, is the essential basis for understanding phenomena such as state intervention and the current phase of imperialism.

Part II

6
The Capitalist State

6.1 Levels of Analysis

The reconsideration of Marxist theory that we have surveyed so far has not itself been generated in a vacuum, but is rather the product of Marxist theory's response to the changing conditions of world capitalism. Thus, while the various schools of thought may have found it necessary to confront abstract theoretical issues, the ultimate objective has been for this work to shed light on the workings of modern capitalism. As a result interest has focused on the increasing economic role played by the state and the relationship of this to the international expansion of capital.

Work on the question of the state can be divided into several types according to the level of abstraction that is involved. Several writers develop abstract propositions about 'the general nature of the capitalist state' (for example, Poulantzas (1973)) and these generally correspond to a treatment which is at the level of the mode of production and which abstracts from the existence of national states. Others, while continuing to analyse the mode of production (abstracting from other modes and therefore from social formations) explicitly introduce the concept of the national state. In consequence, unlike the first type of analysis, they explicitly introduce the idea that the capitalist state, as a national state, has relations (antagonistic and cooperative) with other capitalist states. At a lower level of abstraction the role of the national state in a world where several modes of production exist is analysed. Finally, the national state may be considered

93

in its concrete forms, the national state of the USA or that of the UK in the 1970s.

In this chapter and the next we follow the first approach; we theorise the capitalist state at the same level of abstraction as the mode of production and while abstracting from national states. In Chapter 9 we study the question of imperialist relations and therefore consider the state as a national state, first at the level of the capitalist mode of production (the relations between capitalist national states) and then at the level of relations between capitalist and other modes of production (uneven development).

Apart from these distinctions there is another which must be drawn. We argue in Chapter 7 that the capitalist mode of production has a history; it can be periodised into stages. At different stages, the state has differing levels of significance. Thus, even when we study the state at the level of the mode of production we must distinguish between those characteristics which apply at all stages of this mode and those which are specific to particular stages. In the present chapter we are concerned with the 'universal' characteristics of the capitalist state. In Chapter 8 we turn to those which are specific to the stage of state monopoly capitalism.

6.2   The State, Capital, and Labour

The issues that we have raised so far and the contributions to debates that we have surveyed have essentially been concerned with *economic* reproduction. For capitalism we mean by this the relations directly associated with the production, distribution and exchange of value. It is significant that such a study, the analysis of the economic laws of motion of capitalism, can be undertaken in abstraction from the social reproduction of class relations as a whole. In short, the economic reproduction of capital and the social reproduction of capitalism are to be distinguished, although the latter both includes the former and is essential for it.

However, our economic analysis would constitute an arid study if it were not developed to be located within an analysis of social reproduction. For while it would be possible to perceive in a general way the conflict of class interests associated with economic reproduction, the expression of these in and their relationship to political and other forms of struggle would be excluded. This raises the problem of defining the relationship between politics and economics in the capitalist reproduction of social relations. We do this by considering the commodity labour-power, whose reproduction is essential for capitalism and which, as we shall see, provides a direct link between economic and social reproduction. In terms of economic reproduction alone, the existence of wage-labour depends upon the production of wage goods to the value of wages and the freedom of the labourer to choose an employer. Analysis of economic reproduction shows how this is brought about through and as part of the aggregate circulation of capital, despite the historical laws and cycle of production associated with capital accumulation. This demonstrates that economic reproduction is logically possible, but only in a formal sense, for the existence of wage-labour presupposes the 'freedom' of the labourer in two senses. First, the (economic) freedom of the labourer to choose an employer is a necessary consequence of the existence of labour-power as a commodity, but it is a freedom that directly ties the labourer to a particular term and quality of imprisonment within the capitalist process of production. Second, the wage-labourer is necessarily free from time to time from the process of production (i.e. unlike the slave, from the direct control of the exploiter). But just as capital accumulation imposes definite relations of production upon the labourer in economic reproduction, so are constituted social relations in capitalist society to be consistent with and preserve economic reproduction, and it is within these social relations that the labourer engages in the production of surplus value. As a result, political relations are constituted in capitalist society and the capitalist state exists to guarantee the reproduction of these social (including economic) relations as a whole.

Saying that the capitalist state exists to guarantee the reproduction of the social and economic relations of capital makes one thing clear immediately. That is, it is a mistake to think of the state as concerned only with political relations or to identify it with the political level. (As Poulantzas 1973) tends to do; see Fine and Harris (1976*a*).) It is a focus for class relations at political, economic and ideological levels *and* its institutions 'intervene' in class struggle at all these levels. Although it makes this clear, saying that the state is the focus for class relations at all levels muddies the water in other respects. For there is the problem of which class relations, and also that of whether, if the state is a focus, the class relations are consequently pre-given and simply act through the state. As to which relations, the most fundamental factor is of course the antagonism of the bourgeoisie and proletariat. But within these bounds the state's role is also determined by intermediate strata such as the 'petty bourgeoisie' and by class fractions such as the financial bourgeoisie as against the industrial bourgeoisie. As to whether class relations are pre-given the answer is clearly that they are not necessarily so. Poulantzas (1973), for example, argues that as a political force the bourgeoisie is not a unity which then acts through the state; instead, its unity is itself formed through the state. This conception is explicitly concerned with the bourgeoisie as a class with a political effectivity and it is wrong to try to derive it from the economic laws of capital. Gerstein (1976), for example, makes such a mistake and argues that the bourgeoisie's requirement for the state to act as unifying force stems from economic competition *per se*. The fact that the general rate of profit is formed through the competition of many-capitals is, for him, sufficient to demonstrate that politically the bourgeoisie cannot act as one unified class 'spontaneously'. This reasoning is however, faulty even if we ignore the fact that political class struggle is not simply derived from economic. For the formation of the general rate of profit is an example of how market forces themselves create the bourgeoisie as a class at an economic level. Out of competition is formed the general rate of profit, the bourgeois measure of the exploitation of the working class by the whole bourgeoisie (abstracting from other classes and strata), so that this competition which is an aspect of economic unity is no obstacle to political unity.

There are however some instances where the economy clearly does have an effect on the role of the state as a unifying force for the bourgeoisie (although it must be remembered that 'unity' here means acting on behalf of the bourgeoisie even against some of its own fractions). For example, Marx's analysis of the Factory Acts shows that in such a case an 'intervention' in the interests of capital as a whole is necessarily undertaken by the state because economic competition prevented the bourgeoisie as a class from adopting it 'spontaneously' (if any one capitalist introduced shorter hours he would be defeated in competition even though it may be in his interest for all to have a restriction of hours). Similarly whereas the formation of the general rate of profit is a market process through which the bourgeoisie shares out surplus value like brothers, crises cause the bourgeoisie to fight each other like 'a band of thieves' so that market processes cannot smoothly effect economic unity through competition. In such a situation if the state intervenes at an economic level, as it does under state monopoly capitalism (see Chapter 8), it is forced to act on behalf of the whole bourgeoisie against the immediate interests of some of its fractions (against, for example, the representatives of small capital). In that sense it is acting as the unifying force of the bourgeoisie. Thus it is not competition *per se* which is the economic basis preventing spontaneous political unity; it is competition in particular circumstances, which forces the state to act in the interest of the bourgeoisie as a whole and in that sense unify the class.

As it stands this remains an abstract analysis of the structure of the capitalist mode of production. It cannot serve to locate the economic laws of motion within social reproduction for that would presume the existence of the formation of the class interests of the bourgeoisie at a more complex level of analysis than has been developed. It would take for granted the existence of the economic interests of the bourgeoisie prior to and independent of social reproduction and identify those interests purely in relation to abstract economic laws. Non-economic social relations would then simply be the super-structural expression of economic needs, while the political interests of the bourgeoisie would be confined to limiting the effects on social reproduction of the struggle generated by economic reproduction. As a result political relations would come to be seen as a simple appendage to economic relations through which the economic interests of the bourgeoisie are guaranteed, subject to the strength of working-class struggle. In contrast to such economistic reasoning it must be emphasised that the location of economic within social reproduction must confront the effect of political relations on the bourgeoisie's economic interests. For example, non-economic social relations can have a direct influence on the conditions and forms of competition. Consider the commodity labour-power. Whether over the cycle of production or in the longer term, the economic conditions under which labour is employed are determined in part by non-economic class relations and struggles (e.g. over labour legislation). This is necessarily true because of the relationship between the wage-labourer as producer and as free individual. What affects one affects the other. Consequently at times the interests of the bourgeoisie as a whole will be represented by concessions to the working class, not simply in order to moderate class struggle, but also as a means by which weak capitals that rely upon cruder forms of exploitation for their survival can be eliminated as is required by the economic laws of motion. But at other times, and depending upon the strength of non-economic class struggle, the bourgeoisie's interest may be represented by a failure to grant concessions so that the competitive process remains more dependent upon the market. (See Chapter 7 for a discussion of the Factory Acts.) What this discussion demonstrates is that political relations are not simply an expression of nor a means for guaranteeing the bourgeoisie's economic interests, but that they play a necessary part in their determination and implementation. Just as the processes of exchange express the laws of production but with particular effects and in particular forms, so the same relationship exists between economic and social reproduction. As we have seen, the concrete expression of economic laws varies according to the relative development of different forms of capital in exchange. Similarly the relationship between economic and social reproduction determines but also depends upon the development of political forms. In both cases, there is no strict one-to-one correspondence between the more abstract and the more complex relationships. However, for particular periods of history, concrete historical developments will produce limits within which capitalism's laws are formed, according to the strength of one fraction of capital as against another and according to the existence of one set of political relations as opposed to another. It is to these questions that we turn in subsequent chapters.

6.3 Theories of Capital and the Capitalist State: a Critique

Elements of the analysis of the previous section are to be found in the work of Holloway and Picciotto (1976) (1977). They emphasise that the real unity of political and economic relations creates the illusion of its opposite, the appearance that the capitalist structure of social relations constitutes economic and political relations as absolutely autonomous spheres of activity. Arguing by analogy with commodity fetishism, they perceive that this illusion is not simply false, for politics can in reality be conducted as if in isolation from economics (just as commodities do exchange as things). But economic reproduction is not independent of and indeed is only possible in conjunction with political reproduction. On this basis, they and Clarke (1977) criticise so-called structuralist theories of the state which draw a distinction between politics and economics at the outset without developing it from a concept of capital. Such theories are for them 'fetishised' (in their words), falling under the trap of the illusion set by the structure of capitalist social relations. However, they elevate their discovery of the unity of social relations into a fetish itself, denying the validity of any theory that draws upon the (real but illusory) separation of politics and economics without specifying how the two are reproduced as a totality. This leads to a tendency to analyse the relationship between politics and economics on the basis of an under-developed (because denied) economics. It is most clear in their idea that capital needs to mobilise counteracting tendencies (rather than seeing them in contradiction with the TRPF) and their support for Yaffe's proposition that the law of TRPF necessarily gives rise to shortages in the *mass* of surplus value available for accumulation as well as a decline in the *rate* of profit (on which see below). Significantly their work provides propositions at such a general level that they are uncontroversial; for example, the proposition that the restructuring of capital associated with the law of the TRPF also involves a restructuring of political relations is uncontroversial but rather empty as it stands.

Holloway and Picciotto's focus on the real illusion of the separation between politics and economics is, however, flawed by the development of state economic intervention in the current period. (For a similar criticism, but one which also argues that the state can only be analysed within a system of national states see Barker (1978).) Here, no matter how it may appear, the unity between politics and economics is no longer concealed as economic events have an immediate political significance (nor is a real illusion maintained of the separation between capital and the state although an illusion of neutrality can be created). We consider the problems posed by these modern developments in Chapter 8.

The attack by Holloway and Picciotto and Clarke against what they call structuralism is difficult to understand. At no point do they argue that capitalism does *not* develop particular structures of social relations combined with particular relations of determination, but on the other hand they are not able to develop an account of the current period of capitalism in terms of such a structure because of their under-developed understanding of economic reproduction. Consequently their criticisms of other writers remain at the methodological level; they are an attack on 'structuralism', a label which they apply indiscriminately. For example, their criticism of Poulantzas (in Clarke (1977). This reaches the lengths of misrepresentation (see Tomlinson (1978)) and is in part misplaced for it is unable to confront his particular interpretation of the historical development of capitalism (as one in which political relations have supposedly become 'dominant', for example) with an alternative in which it can be located.

If these authors' emphasis on the real unity between political and economic reproduction is flawed by an inadequate conception of the economy, there are others who misunderstand the unity because of an overemphasis on the economy. Both neo-Ricardians and Fundamentalists confront state economic intervention with their respective ready-made economic theories to which political relations are a simple adjunct. For neo-Ricardians, best exemplified by Gough (1975), the major preoccupation is with those factors that influence the rate of profit. In the case of state (economic) intervention and political relations, as in other areas, these are reduced to their quantitative effects on the rate of profit. It is a simple exercise to extend the state's role to include economic functions which supplement its traditional political and ideological roles. For example, it is argued that the lower the level of welfare services, the higher the level of wage taxation, or the higher the productivity in public employment, the greater will be the rate of profit, just as the rate of profit rises if wages fall or productivity rises in the private sector. The effects are identical and directly comparable even if they are produced more or less indirectly. By the same token state organisation of infrastructure, etc., may be explained by the more efficient (i.e. less costly) provision of a healthy, educated and compliant workforce in general conditions conducive to production than could be provided by a competitive and anarchic provision by private capital.

Such an effortless extension of the role played by private capital to the state's economic role is possible for neo-Ricardians because of their commitment to a concept of undifferentiated labour-time, of exploited labour in general. As a result, economic relations are extended to social relations as a whole in the formation of a simple unity whose fundamental mediating link is the aggregate and common effects on the rate of profit formed.

With Gough, this produces a certain amount of confusion. For, appealing to Poulantzas, he relies upon a separation of politics and economics into relatively autonomous spheres of activity. But the very existence of state economic intervention in the neo-Ricardian framework implies that this separation cannot be maintained as the state acts as capitalist (in nationalised industries), produces 'for' capital (infrastructure) or 'for' labour (welfare services), provides employment (state expenditure) and varies wages (taxation, incomes policy and the 'social wage') so that political and economic struggle become indistinguishable. In so far as the state has autonomy, this, it is argued, is related to its dependence upon the outcome of class struggle and not to its dependence upon the economic laws of motion of capitalism (which are in any case denied except for passing reference to combined and uneven development). As a result the cyclical and secular determinants of state economic interventions are located simply in terms of economic efficiency for capital or as a response to political and economic pressures. In particular Gough puts forward the common argument that the state is committed to full employment as a result of the political demands of the working class. On this, a complete theory of state intervention is erected by neo-Ricardians. Full employment has the effect of increasing the strength of the working class in distributional struggle, thus threatening a fall in the (market price) rate of profit. Consequently the state must at times pursue policies that increase unemployment, representing capital's interest by reducing the strength of the working class in wage bargaining. Of such are crises made and they fundamentally must involve a political and economic defeat of the working class in accepting increased unemployment and lower wages before accumulation can be renewed.

Fundamentalists, locating the contradictions of accumulation within the confines of production, preclude an integration of the state's economic interventions in the complex formation of those contradictions just as exchange and distribution are excluded from their concept of the law of the TRPF. Rather the state becomes a means by which contradictions may be expressed as an *external* response to the contradictions of production. Unlike neo-Ricardians, Fundamentalists arc ablc to draw a clear distinction between economic and political relations by associating the former implicitly with the aggregate circulation of capital (although the basis for political relations is otherwise undefined except as a means by which the interests of capital as a whole may be represented). As such the distinction can be drawn between political and economic struggle and demands. Now for Yaffe (1972) the law of the TRPF gives rise to a tendency for crises, the effect of which would be an increase in unemployment. This is possible without social crisis as long as working class political struggle is not subsequently intensified. Otherwise, he argues, the state is committed to full employment, increasing state expenditure to guarantee aggregate demand and maintain employment. In doing so, it produces a further contradiction or, rather, transforms the contradiction inherent in capital and expressed in the law of the TRPF. It transforms this because the growth of state expenditure itself further intensifies the tendency of the rate of profit to fall and the contradiction therefore takes the form of the state, in attempting to overcome crises, merely intensifying the source of crises and thereby underpinning their inevitability. This occurs because state expenditure must be financed by the taxation of surplus value produced by capital, since state expenditure (except for the operation of nationalised industries) is itself unproductive of surplus value. An increase in state expenditure must imply a reduction in the proportion of any given mass of surplus value which remains in the hands of capital and is available for accumulation: it must, that is, reduce the rate of profit further. A similar view is adopted within the Fundamentalist framework by Gamble and Walton (1976), but for them the primary contradiction which results from the state's supposed commitment to full employment is an intensification of inflation (and consequently of generalised social instability) as state credit expands without drawing upon declining profits. Thus, drawing upon a theory of economic reproduction and a location of this within social reproduction, in sharp contrast to neo-Ricardianism, Fundamentalists arrive at remarkably similar conclusions. The state is seen as being committed to full employment but is prevented from achieving its objective by the necessity of crises (rather than an intensification of distributional struggle). Both neo-Ricardianism and Fundamentalism therefore draw upon an understanding of the current period of capitalism and the state's role within it that has a close affinity to orthodox Keynesiansim. Their major difference is that the state exercises its Keynesian policies on behalf of capital as opposed to a neutrally conceived nation or society in the orthodox theory. It follows that neither theory adequately confronts the relationship between capital and the state either in general or in the context of the current period of capitalism. It is to this last question that we turn in Chapter 8.

7
Periodisation of Capitalism

7.1 The Principles of Periodisation

The idea that present-day capitalism differs in a significant way from that of earlier periods plays an important role in the political strategies of workers' parties and in the theoretical study of capitalist societies. This stage is given various names – late capitalism, monopoly capitalism, imperialism, state monopoly capitalism – and, having named it, several writers have studied aspects of it in relation to particular concrete societies. Prominent among recent studies along these lines are those of Braverman (1974), Poulantzas (1973) (1975) and Mandel (1975), and each presents us with valuable insights. It is, however, rare to find any consideration of what is meant by a stage of a mode of production. Since, in these writings, we only meet the concept of the stage in its applications to concrete social formations it is difficult to separate the concept from the concrete history of the societies to which it is applied. Indeed Poulantzas (1975) claims that it is not possible to have such a concept. For him only concrete social formations may be considered to have a history divided into stages.

Such studies suffer in general from a failure to distinguish between two methods of periodising history. One is to think of stages as highly abstract concepts; stages of a mode of production. The second is to think of them as very complex concepts; stages of social formations. The distinction has been explained above (Chapter 1).

We consider that the workings of social formations can only be understood as the concrete effects of development of the

104

mode or modes of production. Similarly the historical progress of social formations can only be understood as the effect of transformations of the mode of production. These transformations include the supersession of one mode by another, the articulation of different modes in the process of transition, *and* transformations *within* a mode of production from one stage to another. In this and the following chapters we concentrate on the movement within the capitalist mode from one stage to another. Unless this is studied it is impossible to consider the general laws of development of capitalism, and Marxists would be confined to studying how particular capitalist societies have developed without being able to base these developments on general laws. Moreover, unless we can show that the laws of the mode of production give rise to distinct *stages* rather than to continuous *trends* we can have no justification for periodising a social formation's history into stages at all. If asked why we say that British society is at the stage of state monopoly capitalism all we could do would be to say that Britain's concrete history shows distinct differences in different periods: but then we may as well distinguish the periods by the name of the reigning monarch (Victorian England) or the newest form of transport (the 'railway age') as is done in bourgeois textbooks, without reference to the Marxist concept of capital.

The definition of a mode of production is based upon a specific set of class relations of production. The existence of these relations of production implies a further constitution of social relations that are preconditions for economic reproduction (production – distribution – consumption) and social reproduction of classes within this mode. Under capitalism, for example, the relations of production are integrated with the processes and relations of exchange and distribution and these together constitute the circulation of social capital. This economic reproduction, in isolation, cannot guarantee nor exist without social reproduction; thus political and ideological relations are necessarily constituted in the capitalist mode with a particular structure of links between themselves and the economy. In contrast, under feudalism economic reproduction is only guaranteed through the *direct intervention* of non-economic relations.

Although a mode of production is thus defined in terms of *specific* relations this does not imply that no change can take place within a mode. The existence of such changes is the necessary precondition for periodisation of the mode of production into stages. But there are two major problems involved in defining stages of the mode. The first is the question of which types of change are involved in the transformation from one stage into another, and how do these differ from the types of change involved in the transformation from one mode to another. The second is the problem of causation; the question of what dynamic or motive force lies behind the transformation from one stage to another. We begin with the second question, for its answer sheds some light on the first. In particular, we wish to show that transformations within the capitalist mode of production, whether defined as movements between stages or not, can be analysed at that level of abstraction at which the concept of the mode of production (as opposed to social formation) is utilised.

Since we are concerned with the periodisation of capitalism, we shall examine the transformation from laissez-faire to monopoly capitalism (even though we have yet to define these rigorously as stages). This transformation can be treated as the effect of the general laws of the accumulation of capital. We begin by noting two things. First, in *Capital* Marx's analysis is at the level of the mode of production, and a social formation (nineteenth-century Britain) is introduced only as an illustration:

> In this work I have to examine the capitalist mode of production, and the conditions of production and exchange corresponding to that mode. Up to the present time, their classic ground is England. That is why England is used as the chief *illustration* in the development of my ideas. . . . Intrinsically, it is not a question of the higher or lower degree of development of the social antagonisms that results from the natural laws of capitalist production. It is a question of these laws themselves, of these tendencies working with iron necessity towards inevitable results. (*Capital*, vol. I, p. 19. Emphasis added.)

Second, even at this level of the mode of production, class

struggle is introduced and its foundations examined. The proletariat's struggle is shown to arise from the processes of production, exchange and distribution under the capitalist mode and, in a stage where the production of absolute surplus value predominates, it takes the length of the working day as its most significant object. The analysis of the struggle over the length of the working day is presented and illustrated in terms of the history of English society, but Marx makes quite clear that the 1844 Act, for example, is the concrete effect of laws of development and class struggle analysed at the abstract level of a mode of production. The details of the 1844 Act 'were the result of a long struggle of classes' and 'developed gradually out of circumstances as natural laws of the modern mode of production' (*Capital*, vol. I, p. 268). For Marx, the class struggle over the length of the working day is a necessary concomitant of the pure, highly abstract, capitalist mode of production itself. Thus we find:

> Our labourer comes out of the process of production other than he entered. In the market he stood as owner of the commodity 'labour-power' face to face with other owners of commodities, dealer against dealer. The contract by which he sold to the capitalist his labour-power proved, so to say, in black and white that he disposed of himself freely. The bargain concluded, it is discovered that he was no 'free agent', that the time for which he is free to sell his labour-power is the time for which he is forced to sell it, that in fact the vampire will not lose its hold on him 'so long as there is a muscle, a nerve, a drop of blood to be exploited'. For 'protection' against 'the serpent of their agonies' the labourers must put their heads together, and, as a class, compel the passing of a law, an all-powerful social barrier that shall prevent the very workers from selling, by voluntary contract with capital, themselves and their families into slavery and death. (*Capital*, vol. I, p. 285.)

Here, in the clearest terms, is Marx's view that forms of class struggle – in this case struggle over the working day – are the necessary result of the relations or production analysed at the highly abstract level of the mode of production.

We note these things at length because they are controversial, for Poulantzas claims that periodisation into stages *cannot* be conducted at the level of the mode of production since class struggle cannot be analysed at that level. He states that periodisation into stages:

> is applied at the level of the social formation, i.e. the forms of existence of a mode of production, in this case the capitalist: it does not derive from the supposed 'tendencies' of the mode of production itself, this being simply an abstract object. It is only social formations that can be periodized, since it is in them that the class struggle is enacted: a mode of production only exists in the specific conditions – economic, political, ideological – which determine its constitution and reproduction. (Poulantzas (1975, p. 48).)

The example we have given indicates that Poulantzas' method differs from that of Marx. Further, since the limitation of the working day is an essential element in the movement from emphasis on the production of absolute to relative surplus value, transformations of the capitalist process of production can be analysed at the level of the mode.

Accumulation under capitalist relations and the class struggle associated with it are then the basic forces determining the transformation of the capitalist mode from one stage to another. As it stands this is too general a statement (but we shall consider it in more detail below). It does not help us to delineate the difference between a new stage and a new mode nor to discriminate between distinct stages of the mode, for clearly, accumulation and class struggle determine in general the developments within capitalism as well as from the capitalist to the socialist mode of production. To distinguish between these two orders of periodisation it is necessary to examine the *effects* of the development of the forces and relations of production. We know the effects which are identified with a change to a new mode of production – they involve basic changes in relations of production. We would not consider a new mode of production to be characterised by a mere change in the form (legal, for example) in which the relations of production are reproduced; we would, however, consider it to be characterised by a change in the possession and control of means of production exercised by producing and non-producing classes.

In contrast to the changes associated with a change in a mode, the effects of the development of the forces and relations of production on the *form* of social relations within a mode define the transformation from one stage of a mode to another. However, even though we have so far stated rather starkly our criterion for periodisation, it is not one that is pulled arbitrarily out of the air. It is produced by the material development of the modes of production themselves. For example, our analysis of capitalism leads us to understand that it increasingly develops the socialisation of production as the historical precondition for socialism. It is the reflection of this in the development of social relations that we will use to periodise capitalism. This we do in this chapter and the next. Before doing so, we observe that such a periodisation will reveal itself through transformations in the methods of appropriating and controlling surplus value. These methods will assume increasingly socialised forms as the socialisation of production progresses. This will be reflected in transformations in the economic relations of distribution and exchange as well as of production itself. These in turn must have associated with them transformations in social relations as a whole; changes in political relations and the form of the state, for example, being a prerequisite for the more fundamental changes. Underlying these processes and associated with them will be the development of new forms and objects of class struggle, as the bourgeoisie attempts to preserve the social reproduction of capitalism, despite the effects of the increasing socialisation of production.

In the next section we demonstrate that our method of periodising capitalism is consistent with Marx's method of periodising feudalism. Since feudalism through its own development historically creates the preconditions for capitalism, it is periodised into successive stages according to the increasing privatisation of the form taken by the relations of production (toward private property) and the increased socialisation of the form taken by distribution (commodity exchange). Thus the general method for periodising modes of production – according to their own material development toward a new mode – is adopted.

7.2 Periodising Feudalism

In his discussion of the 'Genesis of Capitalist Ground-Rent' in *Capital*, vol. III, chapter 47, Marx analyses three distinct stages in the feudal mode of production. These appear as differences in the institutional arrangements through which surplus labour is appropriated – at one stage labour rent is the institution, later it is rent in kind and at a still more advanced stage it is money rent. The differing forms of appropriation are accompanied by differing institutional forms of control; in the labour rent stage the compulsion to perform surplus labour is physical coercion, with rent in kind comes legal (contractual) coercion, and with money rent the coercion is exercised through legal and market price relations, contracts fixed in money terms. But the important thing about these different stages is that the mode of production remains the same in each. The relations of production are invariantly characterised by an owner of land who is a non-producer, by possession of land in the hands of the direct producer and ownership and possession of the instruments of production by the direct producer. In each they are characterised by appropriation of surplus labour by the owner of land so that the whole of the surplus comprises revenue as rent (or, in some cases, rent and taxes) rather than profit. These particular relations of production determine the pace and character of the development of the forces of production although the development of the forces of production has effects on the relations of production, leading eventually to their dissolution. Moreover, these relations of production give rise to a specific structure of political and ideological relationships characterised at each of the first two stages of the feudal mode by extra-economic coercion to ensure the production of an economic surplus – whether this coercion is by physical force (in the stage of labour rent), or legal enactment (in the stage of rent in kind).

Thus in comparing the stage of rent in kind with that of labour rent Marx argues:

The transformation of labour rent into rent in kind changes nothing from the economic standpoint in the nature of ground rent. The latter consists, in the forms considered here, in that rent is the sole prevailing and normal form of . . . surplus-labour. This is further expressed in the fact that it is the only surplus-labour, or the only surplus-product, which the direct producer, who is in *possession* of the labour conditions needed for his own reproduction, must give up to the *owner* of the land, which in this situation is the all-embracing condition of labour. (*Capital*, vol. III, p. 794.)

The third stage, money rent, is somewhat different. Although it still involves the same basic relations of production and the domination of these relations over the forces of production, at this stage we can see the seeds of the dissolution of the feudal mode based upon the 'natural economy' of feudal agriculture. But it is still a stage *within* the feudal mode: 'the basis of this type of rent, although approaching its dissolution, remains the same as that of rent in kind'. (*Capital*, vol. III, p. 797.)

Thus, according to Marx, the feudal mode of production passes through various stages in its movement to capitalism. Associated with each transformation of the form taken by rent is a new structure of social relations upon which social reproduction is based. These relations embody new forms of the basic feudal relations of production, these forms maintain the basic relations but equally promote new forms of class struggle. In passing, it should be observed that new objects of class struggle are created and at various stages these can either promote the transformation to the next stage (the demand for economic freedom from extra-economic coercion, for example), or lead to a struggle against the relations of production themselves.

The fact that Marx does periodise the feudal mode into stages renders incomprehensible Poulantzas' assertion (1975, p. 44) that 'The CMP exhibits the peculiarity, as compared with "pre-capitalist" modes of production, of being characterised by two stages', with its implication that feudalism cannot be periodised into stages (and for him an inconsistent lapse into talking of the periodisation of a mode rather than of a social formation).

Having considered the principles involved in periodisation and illustrated them in terms of Marx's periodisation of feudalism we now turn to the periodisation of capitalism. In this chapter and the next we examine its stages while abstracting from the existence of national states. In this we follow the method adopted by Marx: 'In order to examine the object of our investigation in its integrity, free from all disturbing subsidiary circumstances, we must treat the whole world as one nation, and assume that capitalist production is everywhere established and has possessed itself of every branch of industry.' (*Capital*, vol. I, p. 581.)

In Chapter 9 we then consider the problem of periodisation when national states are explicitly considered, and the discussion there centres on the problem of imperialism.

7.3   *Laissez-faire* Capitalism

Our basic principle for periodising the capitalist mode of production then is to examine how capitalism's socialisation of production brings about distinct stages involving restructuring of the social relations of reproduction. We shall identify three stages, *laissez-faire*, monopoly and state monopoly capitalism, but our main concern is with the third. Accordingly we consider the others in order to demonstrate the principles of periodisation and to contrast them as stages with state monopoly capitalism. In addition it should be remembered that these are principles of periodisation, so that in concrete history phenomena associated with one stage will co-exist with those associated with the predominant stage. In its *laissez-faire* stage, capitalist production is socialised in its most under-developed form, as a community of commodity producers. As a result of its formal adoption from feudalism of unchanged techniques of production (see Marx's 'appendix' to *Capital* (1976), and also Marglin (1974)), capitalism is characterised by the production of absolute surplus value and accumulation takes the form of concentration. Accumulation provides for increasing productivity through the internal reorganisation of each given production process, thus reaping the benefit of the cooperation and division of labour over the stage-by-stage working up of the commodity produced. This capitalist development of the feudal methods of production does involve the production of relative surplus value, for productivity is increased as the manufacturing system grows. But the production of relative surplus value involved does not correspond to that associated with the growth of the use of machinery, which has as its result the expulsion of living labour, as machines displace workers from the production process. Rather the growth of employment is guaranteed with the accumulation of capital, except with those capitals that are competitvely eliminated. Class struggle associated with this form of the production of relative surplus value is based on the limited effects it has upon the worker, depriving him as it does of the range of skills required to produce a complete commodity rather than part of it in cooperation with others.

The primary contradiction at this stage is that the production of absolute surplus value has limitations imposed upon it by working class militancy which is in turn stimulated by that accumulation itself. For, as long as the production of relative surplus value is restricted to the limits of manufacture, productivity can only grow as fast as the accumulation of capital (through concentration not centralisation), while the growth of the labour force is also in proportion to the accumulation of capital. It follows that the production of surplus value must increasingly come to rely upon the lengthening of the working day, as the avenues to accumulation through productivity increase and wage cuts are closed off. In addition, the form taken by crises in exchange is dominated by the movement of commodity capital and commercial capital to the extent that it develops, giving rise to appropriately named *trade* cycles (whose basis nevertheless remains the contradictions of production).

The ideal forms of the political relations (and this is clearly true of ideological relations also) associated with *laissez-faire* capitalism are those that minimise the economic freedom of the working class. It can be too readily assumed that the establishment of wage-labour heralds the rights associated with freedom of exchange, but these are rights that have to be won in class struggle. The restriction of those rights best

serves the production of absolute surplus value and is best
served by the lack of working class political representation. It
has as its effect the localisation of capitalist relations, particularly in the competition for labour-power, and the corresponding localisation of political power with the central state
restricting rather than enforcing the granting of reforms to the
working class. In Britain, this is illustrated by the New Poor
Law of 1834 with its legislation for settlement and removal,
which, combined with the continued reliance on local relief –
a burden on local rate-paying capitalists – reinforced the
parochial character of capital and obstructed the development of legislation for health, education and factory conditions. (For some analyses of the operation of the New Poor
Law, and a useful bibliography of work in progress see Fraser
(1976).)

The class struggle associated with this period was, as it had
to be, unmediated confrontation between classes whether in
the factories or on the streets. In so far as the bourgeoisie
alone were systematically organised, through the organs of
state power, working class riots were the most open expression of working class militancy. But the systematic organisation of the working class around a programme for political
and economic emancipation promised grave dangers for the
bourgeoisie, unless they could be accommodated through a
restructuring of capitalist social relations.

7.4   Monopoly Capitalism

Monopoly capitalism heralds historically the first full de
velopment of the capitalist laws of motion. The individual
production process is revolutionised through the introduction
of machinery in place of living labour so that technology is no
longer based on the refinement of the techniques inherited
from feudalism. Now for the production of absolute surplus
value and manufacture Marx observed that the lengthening of
the working day by individual capitalists appeared to be
against the interests of capital as a whole, since the resulting
physical destruction of the workforce (including women and
children) increased the cost of reproducing labour-power by
reducing the length of life of workers. But the coercive forces

of competition external to the capitalist made a limitation of the working day impossible without social intervention, i.e. by the state external to economic reproduction. However, no such stimulus to state intervention from capitalists could develop until the advent of machinery. For then the lengthening of the working day forms an object of competition between capitalists as well as between classes. On the one hand small capitalists may support a limitation of the working day to render large-scale fixed capital idle and hence uncompetitive. On the other hand the limitation of the working day can at times act against the interests of small-scale backward capitalists, who continue to rely upon the extensive exploitation of their workers through long hours and low wages. Thus, large-scale capital can also support the limitation of the working day in order to weaken small capitals and take them over in a process of centralisation. With machinery, therefore, capitalist interests in support of the limitation of working hours develop alongside those of the working class. This is reflected in the history of the Factory Acts in Britain, for the legislation developed and was implemented according to the conjuncture of class forces that support the working class's struggle for limitation of working hours.

But machinery does not simply stimulate the Factory Acts. For machinofacture accelerates over manufacture the minimum capital required to produce at sufficiently high levels of productivity. This requires the accumulation of capital to be accomplished through its centralisation, the gathering of many capitals into the hands of a few. It has as its immediate effect the centralisation of labourers in ever larger numbers at the point of production; it requires the breaking down of local labour markets and the creation of freedom of exchange for labour-power.

The consolidation of the phenomena associated with the centralisation of capital characterises the stage of monopoly capitalism. The organisation of workers in increasing numbers in the factories creates the material basis for the formation of trade unions and revolutionises the forms taken by class struggle. New objects of class struggle are created centring on the continual revolution in working conditions and the expulsion and de-skilling of living labour that occur even during periods of prosperous accumulation. However, the monopoly stage of capitalism has its most obvious reflection in economic reproduction through the increasingly socialised forms of the control and appropriation of surplus value.

We consider control first, but note that control of the production process is not an undifferentiated concept. It is distinguished from *possession* in that the latter refers to the actual operation of the means of production and is exercised by the direct producer – under capitalism, the collective worker – whereas *control* refers to the bringing together of means of production and labour-power for the production of values (under capitalism) in a particular manner (appropriate to the production of surplus value under capitalism). Thus control is a more global concept than possession but it has different levels. We do not divide the levels of control arbitrarily but according to the structure of the circulation of individual and social capital, as it is money, productive and commodity capital. Process control refers to the control of particular production units and is concerned with matters such as the speed of the production line and the immediate issues involved in the adoption of new techniques. Accounting control refers to the control, usually thought to be exercised at the level of the firm, of choice of product, choice of technique (including integration of plants or production units), and matters which directly involve the relationship between the particular capital and aggregate capital – matters such as sales and financial policy. Financial control, or control of disposition, is control of particular capitals through the agency of money-capital in exchange. The credit system, for example, is an agent of financial control which dominates the lower levels of control by its role in determining the allocation of capital across the whole economy (while remaining itself subject to the law of value).

The stage of monopoly capitalism is marked by new forms of socialisation of each type of control, symptomatic of which is the mechanism of exchange relations. The development of process control is marked at this stage by the form known as 'the separation of ownership from control' with the growth of a managerial stratum whose formal renumeration is by wages. Accounting control is marked by the existence of monopolies and trusts which increasingly socialise the process of price formation and allocation of market shares. The development of financial control is marked by the existence of a sophisticated credit mechanism for which money-capital itself becomes socialised as a commodity. An integrated system of banks and stock exchanges dominates the distribution of money-capital. These forms of control are interrelated – the development of the credit system being fundamental to the development of monopolies and these, in turn, being the basis for the growth of the managerial stratum. But they are only new *forms* of control. Control of the production process remains in the hands of capital – represented by the owning and non-producing class – and capital is, as under all forms of capitalism, essentially social capital, a social relation. At the monopoly capitalist stage, however, the forms of control correspond more closely than previously to the real social nature of capital; the existence of the credit mechanism ensures this.

Corresponding to the new forms of control at this stage there exist new *forms* of appropriation of surplus value. The credit mechanism ensures that a greater proportion of surplus value takes the form of interest revenue, so much so that appropriation at this stage takes a form qualitatively different from that under *laissez-faire* where profit-of-enterprise predominates.

These features of monopoly capitalism were pinpointed by Marx in his brief comments on the development of joint-stock companies:

> capital, which in itself rests on a social mode of production and presupposes a social concentration of means of production and labour-power, is here directly endowed with the *form* of social capital (capital of directly associated individuals) as distinct from private capital, and its undertakings assume the *form* of social undertakings as distinct from private undertakings. . . . Transformation of the actually functioning capitalist into a mere manager, adminis-

trator of other people's capital, and of the owner of capital into a mere owner, a mere money-capitalist. Even if the interest which they receive include the interest and the profit-of-enterprise, i.e., the total profit . . . this total profit is henceforth received only in the *form* of interest, i.e., as mere compensation for owning capital that now is entirely divorced from the function in the actual process of reproduction, just as this function in the person of the manager is divorced from ownership of capital. Profit thus *appears* (no longer only that portion of it, the interest, which derives its justification from the profit of the borrower) as a mere appropriation of the surplus-labour of others, arising from the conversion of means of production into capital. (*Capital*, vol. III, pp. 436–7. Emphasis added.)

All this is treated by Marx as being predicated upon the development of financial control in this new stage; the development of stock exchanges and other parts of the credit mechanism. (On finance capital see Hussain (1976) and Thompson (1977).) However, the transformation of economic relations is not all that is involved. The development of the monopoly stage of capitalism requires that working class struggle for the limitation of the working day prove successful. This presupposes the political representation of working-class interests and can have the additional effect of moderating class struggle. In Germany this was achieved through the Bismarckian dictatorship (see Dawson (1891), for example). In Britain it was accomplished through the rise of liberal capitalists agitating for reforms that would benefit themselves (as a means of competition against *laissez-faire* capital) as much as their employees. In addition the nineteenth century saw the transition from the stage of *laissez-faire* to monopoly capitalism reflected in a transformation in the form of state power. Legislation on all reforms centred around a relationship between central government and local authority that was successively restrictive, permissive and compulsory as monopoly capital wrested political and economic control from parochial capital. This was not limited to a geographical process, but was also sectoral. The uneven passing and application of labour legislation (factory inspectors could be carefully appointed quantitatively and qualitatively, magistrates were often local employees) represented at times a compromise, at other times a true reflection of divided interests among the bourgeoisie according to the particular conditions of competition between and within classes.

8
State Monopoly Capitalism

8.1 The Socialisation of Economic Reproduction

Before identifying the features of this third stage it is necessary to consider how it is the product of the contradictions associated with monopoly capitalism; its relationship to the forms of class struggle, crises and social relations that develop with the earlier stage. To a limited extent we have already made an analysis of the relationship between crises and monopoly capitalism by consideration of the role of credit over the cycle of production (see Chapter 5). On the one hand the development of the credit system encourages the over-expansion of credit and thereby intensifies violent changes in production over the cycle as collapses occur in both financial and merchant capital, intensifying competition between these and industrial capital. The economic crises of capitalism take on a more violent and threatening character, potentially stimulating working class pressure for the overthrow of the system. For the capitalist class as a whole, the necessity of overcoming these violent eruptions is increased, associated as they are with growing working-class strength and organisation. On the other hand the predominance of interest revenue as the form in which surplus value is appropriated under monopoly capitalism is related to the law of the TRPF and its counteracting influences: 'Since profit here assumes the pure form of interest, undertakings of this sort are still possible if they yield bare interest, and this is one of the causes, stemming the fall of the general rate of profit, since such undertakings in which the ratio of constant capital to the variable is so enormous, do not necessarily enter into the equalisation of the general rate of profit.' (*Capital*, vol. III, p. 437. See also p. 240.)

The development of the credit system and the existence of profit in the pure form of interest represents part of a developing division of 'labour' among capitalists. Just as the immediate control of capital is divided as it passes in its circuit through its various forms, so the division of control within each phase of the circuit develops. Within process control of productive capital, for example, a large managerial stratum relying on a hierarchy of command and responsibility is created. Furthermore the allocation of labour to these functions is itself socialised on the basis of the wage system. It concerns not only intermediate strata, the so-called new petty bourgeoisie of managers, but also stratification within the working class (foremen, charge-hands, skilled expert workers), giving rise to an aristocracy of labour. (This concept is to be distinguished from that of Lenin and Engels which refers to a world division of labour.) The interests of this labour aristocracy are easily identified with the limitation of working-class struggle to the aims of political democracy (for example, abolition of property qualifications for franchise) and social reformism (to moderate economic conflicts and promote meritocracy). Monopoly capitalism is characterised as a stage then in which there develops an intensification of class struggles over economic crises. These struggles are confined within limits compatible with the reproduction of capitalist social relations as a whole by the development of struggle for political democracy as a means to social reform. The partial 'resolution' of these contradictory tendencies that both promote and moderate class struggle under *monopoly capitalism* is to be found in the development of the economic role of the state. The state's predominance in economic reproduction is the distinguishing feature of *state monopoly capitalism* (SMC), the latest stage of the capitalist mode of production. It represents an even higher level of the socialisation of the relations of production than previous stages and is characterised by a new highly socialised mechanism for the control of production. Whereas under earlier stages the dominant social mechanisms for controlling production were the coercive forces of market exchange and the credit system, at this stage state 'intervention' is the predominant mechanism. A direct relationship is created between economic and social reproduction rather than the state simply creating the social conditions in which economic reproduction takes place. The state, however, does not simply replace the existing relations of economic reproduction but exists together with them in a complex relationship thereby transforming their social significance as a consequence of its direct 'intervention' into the circuits of capital.

Our method is to identify a stage by its particular forms of economic reproduction (although these are connected with the corresponding forms of social relations and their contradictions). For SMC consider first the forms in which capital controls production. In financial control the state 'replaces' the private credit system as the dominant agency through which capitalist accumulation is regulated. The mechanisms accomplishing this are complex and varied, but the simplest is state control of the credit system itself both in the sense of controlling private credit through monetary policy and of distributing state credit to particular sectors. This, in turn, is linked to and supplemented by the development of the tax/subsidy system which affects the distribution of financial resources, even if their primary function is or appears to be different (for example, indirect taxation is a socialised form of accounting control since it divorces the market prices of commodities from their prices of production). State intervention in financial control does not originate with SMC, for the ratification of the social existence of money is an intervention at least as old as capital itself. Under capitalism it has direct effects on the level of credit and its distribution. But the substitution of state for private credit raises the significant possibility of transforming the role played by credit as interest-bearing capital. For its basis is no longer directly linked to private profit-making (or more accurately, maximum surplus value appropriation in the form of interest). As we shall see, state credit may be advanced to temper the rhythm of the cycle of production – an action beyond the scope of private capital – and this corresponds to the socialisation of production in which the state acts in conjunction with the market as a mechanism of financial control. Even though the state operates within the areas of financial control and accounting control (through indirect taxation or pricing policy for example) in the circulation of total social capital as well as of individual capitals, it cannot monopolise control even of individual capitals. It can, however, monopolise control of particular capitals in the case of nationalisation since nationalisation involves controlling the operations of the capital throughout the spheres of exchange and production. In this case the state has complete financial control, since it completely replaces the credit system as the *ultimate* source of finance (although this finance itself is ultimately determined by the state's ability to obtain surplus value). The state also has complete control in the sense of accounting and process control – so complete that the state can remove these operations from market competition (setting subsidised prices and maintaining unprofitable employment). This again reflects the development of the state (in conjunction with the market) as the agency through which production is socialised.

Associated with the new form of control, state control, under state monopoly capitalism there exists a major new form of appropriation. Surplus value is at this stage to a large extent appropriated through taxation and this is a form which has no significance under earlier stages of the capitalist mode. In previous stages capital appropriates surplus value by exchange (of money for labour-power and commodities for money) with labour. Then there is no legal compulsion involved in the appropriation. Under taxation, legal compulsion (supported by ideological and political pressures) forces workers and capitalists to transfer money to the state in order that the state shall appropriate surplus value. The state, of course, does not appropriate surplus value for its own sake. As the legal owner of large sectors of capital (nationalised industries) and the controller of privately owned sectors it disburses this revenue by throwing it back into the circuit of capital, by making it available for accumulation as capital (apart from those parts of tax revenue which are used for marginal redistributions of wage revenues and for the production of welfare services). Thus, under state monopoly capitalism, the circuit of capital remains with its essential characteristic, self-expansion. But the surplus value which is the basis of this self-expansion is now appropriated and thrown back into the circuit in a new form, taxation (and credit and subsidies). This new form exists side by side with the other capitalist forms of appropriation based on free exchange, but these other forms are themselves transformed under state monopoly capitalism. Thus the competitive determination of the value of wages through the market and free collective bargaining is modified by state intervention in distributional struggle. An incomes policy, in other words, modifies exchange relationships and introduces an element of legal compulsion. It does so in conjunction with state control of taxes, both representing increasingly socialised forms of the capitalist mode of appropriation (of surplus value). In addition the state's interventions into the credit system alter the balance of competition in the supply of, and demand for, money-capital. The result is that the competitive struggle, between fractions of capital over the appropriation of surplus value as interest or profit-of-enterprise, becomes increasingly socialised through the state.

8.2 Political Transformations

So far we have discussed in general terms the socialisation of economic reproduction associated with SMC. Under capitalism we have also seen how the structure of social relations creates the illusion of a separation between economic and political struggles and there is a strong tendency for struggle to be confined to economic issues. This tendency to economism provides a powerful basis for bourgeois hegemony in social reproduction. However, the features which we have identified as characteristic of SMC have by themselves a tendency to weaken the basis of economism. For the state, which primarily embodies political relations, becomes *directly* involved in economic struggles. In previous stages, struggles over wages or redundancies need not involve the state for they concern exchange and production relationships which directly involve only employers and wage-earners. In particular instances, of course, the state may in these earlier stages be drawn into the struggle, but the point is that under SMC the state cannot avoid direct involvement in all forms of economic struggle. At the stage of SMC the immediate protagonists against the working class in a struggle over wages, for example, are the state institutions which administer, and in which are determined, income and taxation policies. This threatens the division between economic, political and ideological struggles upon which bourgeois hegemony in earlier stages is based; since the state not only intervenes as an economic agent, it is also a crystallisation of ideological, economic and (primarily) political relations. A struggle for wages or over other economic issues would have a tendency under SMC to raise political issues immediately; the question of control of the state and its class nature. It is to overcome this danger that a political transformation is a necessary aspect of SMC.

This transformation may take several concrete forms but in all cases it involves building a system where the political struggle of the working class is contained. Its most developed form is the establishment of bourgeois social democracy so that political parties based on working class support become part of the state apparatus. This enables the working class to obtain the appearance of political power so that the question of control of the state which arises from economic struggles under SMC does not necessarily lead to a political struggle for real control. It enables policies to be pursued in the interests of capital even when their adoption is in response to immediate working class demands – welfare expenditure for example. Most important it can at times defuse economic struggle itself by demanding sacrifices in order to maintain a spurious 'political power'.

But these changes should not be seen merely or even primarily as of ideological significance – maintaining the illusion of the neutral state in circumstances when the class character of the state may be revealed by its extended economic interventions. For while the stage of SMC is characterised by a weakening of the separation between economic and political struggles, the integration of working class struggle into social democratic institutions creates the material conditions for that struggle to be confined to limits compatible with capitalist social reproduction. This is accomplished by divorcing the locus of economistic struggle from the point of production (where for SMC the strength of the working class would inevitably lead to political and ideological crisis) and giving it expression in the institutions of the state.

As we have seen earlier (Chapter 6) these developments in SMC have themselves bred confusions in Marxist analyses of class struggle. The politicisation of economic struggles leads Gough (1975) to identify and confuse political and economic relations, arguing that they constitute a simple structure in which the balance of class power is decisive for determining the rate of profit. Economic demands can be gained as much through political as through economic struggle, since in his view there is a fusion of the 'social wage' (social services) and money wage to form an aggregate level of wages which is determined through political conflict. This suggests a strategy for class struggle based on an ideology that supports the bourgeoisie, one in which the 'social wage' can be seen as a political *quid pro quo* for reducing wages. But in fact it is precisely because the 'social wage' and money wages are entirely different categories that they give rise primarily to different levels of struggle, political and economic respectively. In general the working class is organised in economic struggle at the point of production, but it can be led to sacrifice that by the spurious comparison of money wages with the 'social wage'. In such conjunctures the state control of money wages and the 'social wage' is accepted: each of these is determined with the intervention of political relations in which the working class is less well organised. (For a criticism of Gough on this score in the context of Britain see Fine and Harris (1976a).)

Holloway and Picciotto (1976) (1977), however, do not follow Gough in simply identifying economic with political struggle so that political struggle is seen as in fact dominant. Instead they emphasise that in fact the working class is erroneously confined to economic struggle and fails to see that in reality economic and political relations are parts of a unity. As we have seen, their understanding of state monopoly capitalism is entirely wrong on this score. There is in fact a definite relationship between the economic and the political struggles which occur and the predominance of state economic intervention solidifies this relationship. The problem is not that there is economic and not political militancy. It is that the economic struggles are not of a revolutionary character and they are related to political struggles of a similar nature: the former are trade unionist struggles, the latter are reformist or social democratic. In consequence Holloway and Picciotto's prescription for working class strategy is empty. It is an appeal for a unification of political and economic struggles which fails to see that they are in any case unified. Its emptiness can be seen by comparing it with the strategy of intensifying economic struggle and building on that struggle an intensification of political struggle; a strategy which involves building on what already exists in each sphere and struggling for a qualitative change in each.

Under SMC, then, the objects of struggle associated with economic reproduction, whether over unemployment or the value of wages, for example, increasingly take the forms associated with state economic intervention – such as the struggle for nationalisation, policies for reflation, against incomes policies and their effects. But the separation of these struggles from the point of production and their incorporation into political relations simultaneously creates the potential for new forms of class struggle over non-economic reproduction, over the conditions under which labour-power is reproduced outside the immediate process of producing and circulating surplus value. In particular the working class is able to struggle directly through political relations for the extension of social reforms and for surplus value to be devoted to them rather than to state controlled capital accumulation. Consequently SMC is to be associated with the rise of social reformism as a force whose effects are materialised in the development of the welfare state, a further point of departure for SMC. For while the state in previous stages makes unproductive expenditures of surplus value (to preserve law and order, for example), these correspond directly to the needs of the bourgeoisie and are only indirectly determined by class struggle.

8.3 State Expenditure

SMC is characterised by a growth in state expenditure and consequently by a growth in employment of wage-labour.

The structure of social relations associated with SMC is such as to moderate class struggle over the control of that surplus value and employment and direct its use in the interest of capital accumulation. Nevertheless, class struggle over the employment and expenditure of the state has a significance beyond its direct political implications pursuant upon the use of political control. For while workers can only struggle against the productive expenditure of surplus value when controlled by private capital, struggles over state control of surplus value include those for the extension of unproductive expenditure (possibly at the expense of productive labour).

Consider nationalisation, for example. Whether in conflict over an extension of nationalisation or reorganisation of existing nationalised industries, the proletarian class interest requires state ownership and control in the context of a transformed state and society and, in principle, its pressure over nationalisation is part of its struggle for such a transformation. Inherently it is a struggle for industry to be subject to workers' control both directly and through control of the state which directs the economy. It is a struggle for state ownership *in general* as a step in the abolition of capital; a step in the development toward a society of associated producers. Within a continuing capitalist society it becomes, however, a struggle for the unproductive expenditure of surplus value on the nationalised industries, an attempt to wrest the control of production from capital in ways that restrict but do not abolish that control (the demand for subsidies, no redundancies, etc.). The bourgeoisie, by contrast, requires state ownership precisely in order to preserve the existence of capitalism and capital. This involves ownership by the *capitalist* state (although, as we have seen, a state based on transformed political relations *vis-à-vis* monopoly capitalism) and it involves an attempt to limit the extension of nationalisation, to have only partial and particular nationalisations. This bourgeois requirement of *limited* nationalisation occurs because the class could not exist as such if all production and exchange were nationalised. In addition, for the bourgeoisie, the nationalised industries are to be operated as capital – their rationale being the production and social accumulation of surplus value within a social formation. The struggle of the opposing classes determines the pace of nationalisation and the manner in which nationalised industries are controlled and operated. In this context it should be recalled that the stimulus to state economic intervention is the increasingly violent nature of crises under monopoly capitalism. That this intervention leads to nationalisation, and is not limited to control over exchange and distribution, reflects the inability of the state to maintain production by capital by these means without control of the production process. If the private restructuring of a bloc of capital cannot be accomplished without an explosion of social conflict, the state may be forced to ensure an orderly restructuring through nationalisation, thereby moderating and transforming the demands for workers' control. On the other hand, not being subject itself to the direct control of financial criteria, state economic intervention that does not encompass control of production may weaken the control of that production by capital as either individual capitals or the workers they employ are cushioned from the direct effects of the coercive forces of competition.

These considerations have implications for the forms of control assumed for nationalised industries. Fundamental to this is the separation of class struggle from the point of production, and its removal within a labour movement represented through the channels of social democracy. But this is based on a chain of command that is structured to preserve production by capital, imposing market criteria of profitability prior to a potential development of political crises. Consider Britain by way of illustration. The day-to-day running of a nationalised industry differs little from that of a private company, with boards of management responding to competitive market conditions. Commercial criteria form the link between these boards and government. The recent insitution of the National Enterprise Board, essentially a state-owned financial holding company, completes the picture, creating a further barrier of capitalist rationality between workers' struggles and workers' control.

Before leaving the question of nationalisation it should be noted that we have analysed it in a manner different from that usually employed by Marxists in the study of state expenditure. The relationship between capital and state expenditure of various types has been the subject of much debate in recent years. (See Gough (1975), Fine and Harris (1976a) (1976b), O'Connor (1973).) The discussion has concentrated on the question of whether state expenditure on welfare services is productive or unproductive. We have argued elsewhere that it is unproductive and that this categorisation is centrally important to an understanding of capitalist relations since it emphasises the dependence of all sectors of the capitalist economy upon the *production* of surplus *value*. But concentration upon this taxonomy fails to come to grips with state expenditure as a whole for it tells us nothing about state expenditure in nationalised industries (a category which in this type of debate is mentioned parenthetically as employing productive labour and is then ignored). The argument of the preceding paragraphs suggests that to understand the difference between nationalised and privately owned industries it is necessary to move beyond the mere classification of both as directly productive of surplus value. One has to consider the forces behind the tendency toward nationalisation.

We have done this by identifying for SMC the role played by the state in resolving class struggle over the control of capital as this is increasingly socialised and subject to violent crises of restructuring. This has important implications for the dynamic of nationalised industries (and state expenditure in general) as well as for the dynamic of nationalisation. For whether, and if so the extent to which, the nationalised industries operate as capital is not determined by the legal and institutional forms assumed by state employment but by class struggle over the control of that production. In general it is in the interest of capital to struggle for that employment to be operated *productively*, for the production of surplus value according to the law of value and subject to its direct effects. In contrast the working-class interest requires struggle against these effects and for the operation of state employment *unproductively* for capital, for the planned production of use-values and the maintenance of employment. Thus it is not the supposedly ill-defined and abstract boundaries between productive and unproductive labour in theory which creates problems for categorising state employment as capital or not, but the concrete struggles within the nationalised industries over the reorganisation of production. Again Britain serves as an illustration, with the failure to coordinate the plans of nationalised industries in the same sector (fuel, transport) and the reorganisations within each corporation reflecting the attempt to impose 'commercial criteria', that is, the forces of competition.

We have argued that under SMC economic reproduction brings into question as a matter of class conflict the productive or unproductive employment of labour by the state. Whichever way this conflict is resolved in a particular conjuncture, the matter never rests there. If nationalisation reimposes productive employment on the workers concerned, they are still in a position to struggle against the effects of capitalist production, as in the private sector. On the other hand successful working-class action to expand unproductive expenditure by the state only wrests from capital the direct control of that expenditure. For unproductive expenditure by the state, other forms of control must be developed by capital to subordinate it both quantitatively and qualitatively to the needs of accumulation, thereby giving a specifically capitalist character to welfare expenditure and welfare production. For example, the reproduction of labour-power as a commodity requires that welfare benefits for unemployment lie below the value of wages. The need for a particular structure of skills influences the hierarchical character of the education system. The general drain of surplus value from accumulation represented by welfare expenditure ensures that the welfare state is subject to severe constraints and far from adequate (as in health services). Institutionally the ability of the working class to struggle for welfare is disorganised as far as possible, with local government subordinated to central government and decision-making removed not only from the recipients and producers of welfare but also from the working class organised as producers.

For some the welfare state simply represents a means for moderating class struggle. For others it is a product of class struggle in which the proletariat makes gains. A third school sees the welfare state as guaranteeing and providing the conditions for social reproduction. This last view is essentially correct but it needs to be related to the particular role played by the reserve army of unemployed in economic reproduction. For this is not simply a product of capitalist accumulation as workers are expelled from the production process, but also a condition guaranteeing the ability to centralise capital (including variable capital). The welfare state represents more than the regulation and maintenance of the reserve army; it provides for the socialisation of the conditions through which it exists (the unhealthy do not become unemployed directly, the unemployed are available for employment rather than existing as domestic servants, etc.). The analysis of this in detail is beyond our scope here.

8.4   The Cycle of Production

State monopoly capitalism is, then, a stage at which the state directly participates or 'intervenes' in the economy. This does not mean the abolition of capital and of the organisation of the economy (and society) on a capitalist basis, but it does mean a change in the forms of that organisation. Surplus value is appropriated but now in the new form of taxation (as well as the old forms of interest, profit on enterprise etc.). The economy continues to be controlled according to the needs of capital, but the agency of that control is now the state (as well as the old agencies of the market and the credit mechanism). Since SMC does not involve the abolition of capital it does not abolish the laws of motion of capital. The law of increasing concentration and centralisation of capital remains valid although the form in which it operates is altered, the law of the TRPF and its counteracting influences remains valid, and the law that accumulation is necessarily punctuated by crises remains although the form of crises and the business cycle is modified. In this section we consider how the analysis of capitalist crises and cycles which we set out in Chapter 5 remains valid with modifications under SMC.

The essential point is that the state actively intervenes to affect the course of the cycle but does not abolish it. This failure to abolish the cycle arises because, in Marx's conception, as long as capital remains the technical (and hence organic) composition has a tendency to rise; and this produces the TRPF and its counteracting influences which, as we saw in Chapters 4 and 5, are the basis of capitalist crises and cycles. Before going on to consider the ways in which the state nevertheless affects the cycle it is illuminating to consider the error made by Keynesianism in thinking that the state can abolish crises. It arises from the view that crises are caused by deficient demand so that the state can always avoid crises by influencing the demand for commodities (demand-management). It ignores the fact that the deficiency in demand merely concerns the form of crisis rather than its cause, that the cause lies in the contradictions of the law of TRPF and the counteracting influences, and that this cause is inherent in capitalist production and can only be eradicated by the abolition of capitalism. In other words Keynesianism ignores the fact that the capitalist state, responsible for the reproduction of capitalist relations, is forced to permit and even at times precipitate crises. For crises are not only disastrous for sections of the bourgeoisie and, of course, the working class; they are also the preconditions for renewed capitalist accumulation (although they never guarantee that renewal) and the capitalist state cannot provide these preconditions in any way which avoids crises. These considerations enable us to see how the state at the stage of SMC affects the cycle of production (or, since crisis is the predominant aspect of the cycle, intervenes in crises).

There are certain forces, elaborated by Marx in *Capital*, vol. III, chapter 15, which are unleashed in crises at all stages of the capitalist mode of production. At the stage of SMC, as we have argued elsewhere, (Fine and Harris (1975) (1976a) (1976c)), the state acts to strengthen these forces when crises break. These forces are in a structured relationship to each other so that some are more fundamental than others. The restructuring of productive capital is the most basic of these processes. It takes the form of speed up and the expulsion of labour both with existing fixed capital and with the adoption of more advanced fixed capital (although the latter is properly part of the accumulation for which crisis creates the preconditions rather than one of the forces within crises). This restructuring of productive capital is the most basic of forces in crises because it is essential for raising the production of relative surplus value and thereby temporarily resolving the contradictions which give rise to crises. On the basis of it other forces develop. The most significant of these at the economic level is a redistribution of revenue toward surplus value (i.e. from labour to capital) and simultaneously an intensification of struggle for surplus value between different sections of the bourgeoisie.

At the stage of state monopoly capitalism the state intervenes to strengthen these processes, both the most fundamental and the derivative. The state intervenes directly in the restructuring of productive capital through its position as an agent controlling the economy at all levels. At the level of financial control the state intervenes in the distribution of surplus value between capitals to foster directly the restructuring of capitals (grants, subsidies, etc., conditional upon the restructuring of the industries which receive them). And where the state has accounting control and process control, as it does in nationalised industries, the state itself carries out the restructuring. Moreover, there is a tendency in crises under SMC for the state to extend its control so that it nationalises (takes over accounting and process control in) more sectors. In these respects the state directly stimulates the restructuring of productive capital. It also intervenes in the processes which indirectly stimulate it, especially distributional struggle between labour and capital. Through taxation, subsidies, and wages policies the state is able, at least temporarily, to influence distribution in the direction required for the restructuring of capital. In crises this generally involves an increase in profit, although as we note below such an increase may also hinder the restructuring of capital. It is instructive to see how this distributional intervention is achieved. Wages policies which push down the value of wages redistribute by pushing the value of wages below the value of labour-power, and also by influencing the value of labour-power itself (the moral and historical element). Taxation and subsidies have effects which are most significant when reinforced by wages policies. A rise in taxes on workers, for example, generally gives rise to pressure for an increase in gross wages to maintain their relation with the value of labour-power so that ultimately taxes on workers fall on capital and are not an instrument of redistribution. An effective wages policy, however, prevents this effect and permits a rise in taxes on workers to be used as a means for redistribution to capital.

The state's economic intervention in crises is also accompanied by intervention in ideological and political struggle. The expulsion of living labour in the restructuring of productive capital and redistribution toward capital are processes which carry the threat of stimulating working class militancy at all levels. It therefore becomes imperative for the bourgeoisie to mount a counter-offensive and the state acts as a focus for this. As we argued in Chapter 6 the state itself acts to form the political unity of the bourgeoisie; it is also responsible for the ideological apparatuses of capitalism under SMC. The state itself, therefore, is instrumental in mounting this ideological and political counter-offensive which is necessitated by the essentially economic requirements of capital in crises. It is this which in a very unspecific manner Holloway and Picciotto (1977) characterise as a 'political restructuring' which arises from the fact that the state is an aspect of 'the capital relation'.

The economic interventions of the state in crises give rise to two particular phenomena which appear as reversals of the historic gains of the working class. The first is attempts to cut its expenditure upon welfare services. Welfare services involve unproductive expenditure so their financing reduces the proportion of surplus value which is available for accumulation as capital; reductions in welfare services, therefore, redistribute surplus value from unproductive expenditure to capital. (It should be noted that this interpretation is quite different from that of Gough (1975), see Fine and Harris (1976a) (1976b).) The second is the strengthening of the capitalistic element in nationalised industries. We saw earlier in this chapter that nationalisation involves an ever present tension between the interests of the working class (which requires nationalisation as a step toward proletarian control of the economy) and those of the bourgeoisie (which requires their operation as capital). In crises the operation of the nationalised industries is transformed so that it conforms more closely to their operation as capital. Criteria of commercial profitability are imposed or reinforced and the expulsion of living labour is forced forward. This can be brought about in a number of different ways, each corresponding to control of capital at a different point in the circuit. First, the direct coercion of market competition can be intensified organisationally by creating competition between nationalised industries themselves, as well as with private capital (in Britain, for example, in the transport and energy sectors, for which the nationalised industries neither have a monopoly nor are integrated under a plan). Second, the relationship between the state and the nationalised industries can be mediated by state institutions committed to financial control and geared to profit-making (in Britain, the development of the National Enterprise Board is an example). This has the further effect of weakening if necessary the political implications of state intervention, as the struggles at the point of production are divorced from political power by the economic rationale imposed by the financial institution. Third, production within nationalised industries which is unproductive – does not operate as capital – can be reorganised as capital (in a sense, a form of primitive accumulation). Here the conversion of unproductive to productive expenditure does not involve the cut in one to expand the other. Rather the reorganisation of production is aimed at redefining the boundaries that divide the sphere of capitalist production from the sphere of social reproduction (in Britain, this is significant for British Railways and the Post Office).

The cycle of production under state monopoly is characterised by an entirely new phenomenon, or, rather, a phenomenon which is in fact very old but which is transformed by state monopoly capitalism. That is inflation. To consider it is to move on from direct consideration of state intervention, but inflation under SMC is nevertheless inextricably linked with the state's role.

In terms of the hierarchy of determination which we discussed in Chapter 1, inflation is a phenomenon which appears on the surface of society and is determined by the interaction of deeper forces; in terms of analytical method, inflation is a complex rather than highly abstract concept. The existence of inflation as a complex phenomenon breeds theories to explain it that rely upon one or more causal factors superficially treated, that is in isolation from or in simple relation to accumulation and economic reproduction. In contrast it should be argued that inflation cannot be reduced to a single determining cause (such as workers' militancy or a bourgeois conspiracy) and only to an *ensemble* of determinants, when these are themselves constructed in a hierarchical relationship to each other. We base our discussion on taking as given the cycle of accumulation and examining how the rhythm of inflation is related to it.

Inflation concerns increases in the price of commodities in terms of money. In Marx's analysis, set out in *Wages, Price and Profit*, the matter is relatively simple. There, for inflation to occur the value of commodities in terms of the money commodity (gold) must rise unless we assume that the prices of production or market prices of commodities in relation to money are above their values to an increasing extent. These value relations provide the conditions and limits within which such aspects of economic class struggle as workers' militancy for a higher value of wages has its effects. Essentially they imply that workers' militancy can raise the value of wages to a limited extent; money wages can be pushed up temporarily without necessarily causing a rise in prices. This analysis can be used to study how the value of wages changes over the production cycle, as competition in the demand and supply of labour fluctuates with accumulation. But it can only be so used if money does take the form of commodity money such as gold. One of the distinguishing aspects of SMC is the transformation of money so that it no longer takes this form. Therefore analysis where inflation is limited by changes in the relative value of the money commodity is not directly applicable in this stage of the capitalist mode.

If changes in the relative value of the money commodity are no longer a limit to the inflation of commodity prices it is equally invalid to suppose that money imposes no limits on inflation. Money does impose limits but instead of arising simply from the relative value of the money commodity these limits arise from the role of money in the circuit of capital. Before examining these limits we should note that many Marxist analyses proceed as if they did not exist. For example, so-called conflict theories (see Harvey (1977)), which are merely a development of Glyn and Sutcliffe's (1972) neo-

Ricardian approach, argue that inflation is determined by the relative strengths of the bourgeoisie and working class in distributional struggle without considering how this process is limited by the role of money in the circuit of capital. Similarly the Fundamentalists' argument, that inflation is the result simply of the state's need to increase the money supply in order to finance its unproductive expenditure, ignores, as we shall see, the role of money as money-capital.

What is the significance of the role of money in the circuit of capital? It is essentially that capital necessarily takes the form of money (money-capital) at one phase of the sphere of exchange and that this money-capital must be equal to the commodity capital with which it exchanges if the circuit is to proceed and be renewed. It follows that if capital accumulation is contracting the money-capital element in the circuit must contract if the unity of the circuit is to be maintained. Marx saw the role of hoarding in this light (see de Brunhoff (1976)). Hoarding involves withholding money-capital from the circuit; a rise in hoards decreases the amount of money which acts as capital and at times when the circuit of capital is contracting can ensure that money-capital is contracted accordingly. Apart from or together with hoarding, inflation acts in a similar manner; for inflation too reduces the 'value' of any given quantity of money-capital. From this point of view, therefore, inflation is determined in accordance with the rate of expansion of the circuit of capital and the rate of hoarding or dis-hoarding. All this assumes that the circuit runs its course smoothly and is expanding or contracting without violent interruption. It involves a paradoxical result, that as the value of the elements of commodity capital declines because of technical progress, the money prices of commodities may rise to reduce the 'value' of money-capital – unless either hoarding withdraws sufficient money-capital from the circuit or accumulation proceeds fast enough to ensure that the total mass of capital in value terms (value of the mass of commodity capital for example) is large enough to be commensurate with the existing money-capital. It follows that the rate of inflation is determined by the relationship between the pace of accumulation and the rate of hoarding (or dis-hoarding and expansion) of money-capital. This relationship can only be explored, however, by distinguishing between the role of credit between capitals in competition and the role of credit between capital and labour (on which see Harris (1976)). For the former credit is only significant in this context when it is advanced and received in expanding the circuit of capital. For then it depends upon the production of surplus value for its function to be realised. From the perspective of the individual industrial capitalist borrowing money (-capital), for example, surplus value must be produced and realised for the interest (and profit-of-enterprise) to be received. However, this cannot be seen as a purely individual act, for the role played by such credit socially is to promote the production of relative surplus value through the centralisation and accumulation of capital. The individual capitalist is an agent in this process, driven by competition with other capitalists to seek credit as a means of centralisation. Whether or not credit as capital expands in disproportion to the circuits of capital depends upon the extent to which the centralisation and accumulation of capital, which it stimulates and promotes, is successfully accomplished. In short the expansion of credit as capital involves a necessary intervention in the circuits of capital to promote their expansion, but presupposes the production and realisation of surplus value if inflation is not to result. In addition, where credit circulates in the circuits as capital, it has the role of money(-capital) even if assuming different forms from gold.

Credit relations are not, however, limited, even between capitals, to the expansion of money as capital. But where they are not, they simply perform the function of easing the circulation of commodity-capital and do not have the effect of expanding the circuits of capital. Put another way such credit exchanges against surplus value already produced and merely anticipates movements of money (when the IOUs are reclaimed). Of course, if a credit note is created and circulates independently as money and subsequently as capital, then capital must expand to maintain balance between production and circulation without inflation (unless an equivalent in money is hoarded). However, it would not be the credit note itself which would be at the root of any inflation. Rather the conditions which allow the possibility of such a credit note to circulate as money (the existence of finance capital or state credit) and the forces which turn this possibility into actuality have to be located in relation to the pace of accumulation as discussed earlier. We return to this below in the context of state credit. In the credit relations between capital and labour, there are two considerations. First, when labour-power is purchased by the capitalist, it has already been seen that credit as capital may be extended to the capitalist to promote centralisation. The more wages are bid up, the more this may be necessary, but higher wages should not be seen as the source of the credit expansion. For it is only through increasing wages, especially during a period of expansion, that capital can be centralised with the less efficient (small-scale) capitals being squeezed between falling output prices and increasing wages. Indeed it can be argued that an over-expansion of capital stimulates inflation at this point, not through permitting wage increases (which it does), but through restricting both the liquidation of inefficient capitals and consequently the increasing production of (relative) surplus value.

In the movement $C'-M'$, where workers purchase means of consumption from capitalists, credit may be granted to workers. But as we have already observed in the inter-capitalist exchange, the credit advanced merely promotes the realisation of an existing mass of surplus value, and is not of itself inflationary. In addition it should be observed that the intervention of credit in this act of exchange may alter the form adopted by exchange of equivalents (and this is also true for the inter-capitalist exchange) with interest falsely appearing to be a 'penalty' for the credit advanced. While for the individual worker this may appear to open a world of freedom (through hire purchase and mortgage), socially it binds the worker closer to capital reinforcing the presure to work (just as for the miner's bond to the company shop). Even where workers themselves advance credit, through savings, this is merely a means by which the value of labour-power is spread over a lifetime, so that the worker is self-sufficient during times of hardship (see Harris (1976)).

It must be remembered that the foregoing arguments apply under SMC because money does not take the form of commodities (gold) with their own value determined in accordance with labour embodied. Money is, at this stage, created by the state (in interaction with the banking system and all forms of financial capital) as an effect of the state's intervention in the credit system. The question then is how the state affects the variations in the circuit of capital which, as we have argued, determine inflation. The state, as argued in Chapter 6, is the focus for the antagonisms between the bourgeoisie and the working class and also for those between different fractions of the bourgeoisie. Its effects on the circuit of capital are determined by those antagonisms.

Consider, first the antagonism between bourgeoisie and working class. One effect of this is the state's intervention to temper the rhythm of accumulation, or in other words the rate of expansion of the circuit as a whole. For it is this class antagonism which ultimately lies at the source of crises and cycles, and the state intervenes to influence these cycles (while not abolishing them). Another effect is the state's influence on hoarding and this arises through the fluctuations in state credit. This credit is the counterpart to state budget deficits and so it is influenced by the working-class struggle to force the state to increase its expenditure to maintain full employment and to maintain social services. It may take the form of bond issues alone or (either directly or indirectly) the creation of money. In either case an expansion of state credit has an influence on hoarding but it is by no means necessarily an inflationary influence. Bond issues absorb money which would otherwise be available as money-capital; they withdraw money from its role as money-capital to the extent that the state uses the money for unproductive expenditure. The creation of money, equally, does not directly increase money-capital in the case where it is spent by the state as unproductive expenditure. The effect of the creation of state credit when the state is forced by the capital/labour contradiction to finance budget deficits is therefore equivalent to an increase in the amount of money which is hoarded ... there is an increase in the amount of money which is spent as revenue rather than capital. Since inflation is associated with a disproportion between money-capital and the circuits, it follows that the expansion of state credit cannot be identified as necessarily causing inflation. Some of this money will eventually enter the circuit of capital as money-capital (as the recipients of this revenue spend it on commodities produced by capital) but then it involves an increase in money-capital which is identical with the expansion of the circuit itself, because it enters the circuit to exchange against and realise surplus value already produced.

This, it should be noted, is in contrast to the position taken by Yaffe (1973). He argues that class struggle ensures that the state necessarily attempts to maintain full employment for political stability (which as we have seen is a false Keynesian view), that this necessarily involves an expansion of state credit in the form of money (again, a false view) and that this necessarily results in inflation because the money expansion does not correspond to surplus value produced. Now given that state expenditure has both productive and unproductive elements, it might seem arbitrary to choose one sector of expenditure as requiring credit expansion and being inflationary rather than another. Yaffe chooses as being inflationary state unproductive expenditure (expanded to maintain employment) since it reduces the surplus value available for accumulation. In contrast, we have argued that it is the expansion of state credit as capital that is inflationary with the reservation that it is so only relative to the pace of accumulation and centralisation (for which state unproductive expenditure does not form the only limit). That Yaffe's argument is erroneous can be seen in a number of related ways. First, it would imply that any luxury consumption by the capitalist class is inflationary since, like any unproductive expenditure by the state, it reduces the surplus value otherwise available for accumulation. In fact the *distribution* of surplus that has already been produced, whether between classes or between productive and unproductive labour, cannot be considered inflationary as such. It must be related to the expansion of money-capital relative to the production of surplus value.

Second, Yaffe does not relate the expansion of state credit to the accumulation process, and in particular to the competition between capitals for money-capital. Rather he merely relates it to the redistribution of surplus value through state credit, ignoring the fact that this can be done without expanding the money supply (through a bond issue which can have the effect of reducing the circulation of money-capital). Once corrected for this erroneous conception of state credit, Yaffe's theory reduces to a monetarist theory of inflation in which the state simply makes the mistake of expanding the money supply faster than the rate of growth.

Third, even within this formulation Yaffe can be seen to be erroneous relative to Marx's categorisation of capital's circuit since he conflates different turnover periods of capital. Marx in Volume II of *Capital* asked how was it possible, in simple reproduction for example, for $C+V+S=M'$ to be realised when only $M=C+V$ was thrown into exchange by the capitalists. The answer is that the $m=M'-M$ already exists in the hands of capitalists enjoying luxury consumption. For expanded reproduction the money-capital in the circuit must also increase either through the production of gold or an advance of credit in its place. Yaffe can be interpreted as making a polar error, puzzling over Marx's paradox in reverse. For him, because M' has emerged from the circuit (on the basis of an expansion of money as credit) but only M has been thrown into the circuit, inflation must result in proportion to the difference between M' and M. But, of course, surplus value has been produced in the movement from M to M'. Yaffe inverts a theory of underconsumption – how can S be realised – into a theory of excess demand – how can m be spent?

Before moving on from the effect on the state of the struggle between the bourgeoisie and the working class, we must consider the nature of wages policy. The state's intervention in the determination of wages has been seen by many as the major aspect of the state's role in inflation. The state presents these policies as attempts to reduce inflation with the implication that all classes will benefit alike from its reduction. In fact wages policies are primarily concerned with redistribution both between labour and capital and between capitals, and in general require for their effect a difference between the rate of growth of money wages (money price of labour-power) and the inflation of other money prices. Wages policies are concerned, that is, with shifts in the value of wages. The neo-Ricardian school, concentrating as it does on distributional struggle, emphasises this redistribution alone so that it appears that the state always acts in the interests of the bourgeoisie by imposing wages policies. Fundamentalists take the view that this redistribution is required by developments in the sphere of production so that wages policies become strengthened in crises in an attempt to finance the restructuring of capital by increasing profits. The Fundamentalist view is based upon the hierarchical relationship between production, exchange and distribution and therefore sees wages policy in terms of the cycle of production and accumulation. But like neo-Ricardianism it does not make clear that wages policy is not always in the interests of capital as a whole and cannot be seen simply as a bourgeois conspiracy. Wages policy is also an effect of and has an effect on competition between capitals. Its effect on competition may be to ensure the survival of capitals which would otherwise be transformed by centralisation, for a reduction in the value of wages enables relatively inefficient capitals to survive. To this extent wages policies are not always in the interest of capital as a whole and may contribute toward inflation by weakening the tendency toward restructuring of capital.

We have not yet, however, examined the relationship between wage struggles and inflation. Before doing so it is necessary to consider state intervention in distributional struggle between classes in isolation from its relation to inflation. Earlier (Chapter 5) it has been argued that there is a tendency for the value of wages to fall below the value of labour-power during a recession as unemployment increases. This is not simply a matter of distributional struggle, but an essential part of the depreciation of (variable) capital, whereby it can be subsequently reorganised both through capital's ability to draw upon the expanded reserve army and through centralisation in the wage goods industries. It follows that the state will intervene through taxation and incomes policies to reduce the value of wages. During a period of expansion, however, it is necessary for wages to have a tendency to rise, not simply because of the increased strength of the working class in distributional struggle as employment increases, but also as a means of centralising capital. If wages are controlled during this period, the effect is to hinder centralisation as the least competitive capitals are maintained in existence by low wages. Thus, it should be observed that the interests of capital as a whole are not represented in every instance by a reduction in the level of real wages (in particular during periods of expansion) as a means of increasing the rate of profit, as neo-Ricardians would argue. In this light, it can be seen that workers' demands for wage increases cannot be considered to cause inflation, and this is not simply because they interact with capital's administration of prices, so that blame cannot be apportioned. The value of wages can rise without an over-expansion of credit and money as capital, indeed this is necessary during a period of expansion. As a distributional struggle between capital and labour, the competitive determination of the level of money wages is not to be discovered in the expansion of state credit as capital or of money capital. However, it should be observed that, because the competitive struggle between capitals in the process of centralisation can intensify inflation, it can lead to an intensification of distributional struggle between capital and labour over the level of real wages, further stimulating state intervention based on the ideology that wage controls lead to a reduction of inflation. Those (neo-Ricardians) who argue in support of this – a direct link between wage increases and inflation – are, while wrong, consistent in their method. For the transformation problem, neo-Ricardians emphasise competition in exchange within classes at the expense of competition between classes in production. For inflation, implicit to their theory is the failure to distinguish between credit as capital and credit in general; with the implication that workers and capitalists equally strive, possibly indirectly, to expand credit in order to ratify increases in revenue (as wages or profits).

9
Mode of Production, National States and Imperialism

9.1 Periodisation of the World Economy

In the previous chapters we have developed a periodisation of capitalism into three stages. We have done this at the level of the mode of production, without considering concrete social formations. Moreover, we have abstracted from the existence of national states so that the periodisation of the capitalist mode at which we arrive is one constructed from the tendencies and contradictions of capital accumulation in general. Now the national state appears to be a simple concept but this is not so. We must ask what distinguishes the national state from the state in general and examine the relationship between it and capital.

The primary function of the state-in-general is to guarantee the reproduction of capitalist social relations – relations which pertain to the existence of capital-in-general. The national state, on the other hand, presupposes the division of social reproduction and also the division of capital into competing blocs (many-capitals). It will be argued below that this division is not a simple one: one cannot assume that capital is divided into national capitals in one-to-one correspondence with national states (a 'British capital' to which corresponds the British state apparatus) and the division of social reproduction is not one which makes the reproduction of nations its main element. Nevertheless the existence of the national state under capitalism is predicated upon the existence of competi-

146

tion between blocs of capitals and the related division of social reproduction. This is to be contrasted with those views which take the national state as the product of 'natural' nations which are defined in terms of unexplained linguistic and cultural characteristics. It is also to be contrasted with those views which see the existence of the national state and its state apparatus only in terms of economic reproduction; for to say that the national state is predicated upon competition between capitals means that the political and ideological roles of its national state apparatus as well as its economic are determined in this way.

In saying this and in what follows (until Section 4) we are continuing to work at that level of abstraction which pertains to the capitalist mode of production. Once we move to a lower level of abstraction it is no longer enough to say that the national state and its state apparatus is predicated upon competition between capitals; it is then a product of the antagonistic articulation between capitalist and other modes of production.

Remaining at the level of the capitalist mode of production we can arrive at a periodisation of capital based upon the reproduction of the world economy. Capital accumulation involves the expansion of capital beyond national boundaries and produces both the internationalisation of capital and international competition. But these take different forms. Initially, whether accumulation is based on the production of absolute or relative surplus value, accumulation of productive capital guarantees that national capitals expand beyond their boundaries in their search for expanded markets to ensure that realisation and completion of their circuit is possible. Thus commodity capital is the first form of capital to be internationalised, and this can be taken as the index of the first stage of the world economy. The development of the credit system which accompanies the predominance of the production of relative surplus value facilitates the internationalisation of financial capital, and this may be considered as its second stage. The intensified production of relative surplus value gives rise to a third stage in which productive capital itself is internationalised with multinational corporations controlling production processes which cross national boundaries. At each of these three stages, the formation of the capitalists' class interest through the national state represents different internal conflicts as the external forces of competition are transformed. For the stage dominated by the export of commodity capital, each competitively weak sector of capital stands to gain through protection, while other capitals in general stand to gain through the import of commodities produced at lower values. The export of financial capital hastens the process of centralisation within each national state, intensifying the conflict between small and large scale producers. Finally, the internationalisation of productive capital divides capitals, not according to their ability to compete on the world market or gain access to world finance, but according to their ability to organise production across national boundaries. Associated with each stage, a section of national and foreign capital have a 'natural' alliance whose interests come to dominate state interventions as the world economy develops.

We have therefore, in principle, a periodisation of the capitalist mode that brings to the fore the transformations of social relations and class struggle which arise from accumulation in general (Chapter 7), and now, in addition, a periodisation of the world economy that is based on the existence of national states and international competition. It could be argued that the two periodisations simply coincide with each other. However, even if this could correspond to the historical development of capitalism as a world system, it could not render the dual principles of periodisation redundant. For the two sets of stages through which capitalism progresses are not united in a simple fashion in which the characteristics of each are added together or necessarily reinforce each other. Consider, for example, three related issues central to the integration of the two periodisations. First, the formation of the bourgeois class interest is on the one hand a product of class struggle associated with a stage of the mode; and on the other hand a product of competition between national capitals at a stage in the world economy. Neither one influence nor the other is a simple product or addendum of the other, but each depends upon the configuration of class alliances constructed, for which there is no objectively determined outcome.

Second, the reproduction of the capitalist mode and the world economy together produce the reproduction of the proletariat in nations and the reproduction of those nations. As the exchange of labour-power becomes increasingly internationalised, whether through emigration, or *gästarbeiter*, again the result depends upon a configuration of class alliances which is not predetermined by the logic of periodisation. Finally, each periodisation has presupposed, except during phases of transition, the existence of each stage in its pure form. But, as theorised in the law of combined and uneven development, the progression of capitalism through its stages produces the co-existence of capitals at different stages of development, and even the co-existence of capitalist with pre-capitalist modes. It is the resolution of these issues that constitutes the study of imperialism to which we now turn.

9.2 Imperialism and Capitalism's Stages

In everyday usage, the word 'imperialism' describes the domination, whether political, economic, or ideological, of one nation by another. It is invariably used pejoratively. As such it is based on nationalist ideology rather than Marxism. It acquires a Marxist class element if amended so that it relates to the domination of some or all of the classes of one national state by the bourgeoisie of another rather than domination of one nation by another. But however amended, the idea of domination across national boundaries is not the main element of the Marxist concept of imperialism. Whereas domination as such is as applicable to ancient Roman society as to modern capitalism, 'imperialism' essentially refers to the relations existing at a certain stage of capitalism. Since Lenin, the Marxist concept of imperialism is primarily the idea of a stage of capitalism. For Lenin, imperialism was seen as 'the highest stage of capitalism' and some modern writers such as Poulantzas (1975) adopt the same perspective, while at the same time subdividing the stage of imperialism into distinct phases to allow for the variations which have been experienced since Lenin wrote. To say that imperialism is a stage of capitalism, however, raises several theoretical questions rather than settling them. Here we examine some of the problems the concept involves.

As suggested in the previous section the concept of imperialism implies an integration of the two processes of periodisation, and therefore involves a level of abstraction more complex than those employed for the periodisations. This is exemplified by Lenin's pamphlet *Imperialism*, which was not a theoretical tract at a high level of abstraction. That it was not written as a contribution to high theory is indicated by its sub-title: *A Popular Outline*, and by the fact that it was written 'with an eye to the tsarist censorship' and therefore had to be structured around the 'admissions of bourgeois scholars'. That it was not concerned with highly abstract concepts but with the complexities of concrete social formations is indicated in Lenin's 1920 *Preface* where he states his purpose as 'to present . . . a composite picture of the world capitalist system in its international relationships at the beginning of the twentieth century – on the eve of the first world imperialist war.' He might as well have added 'and the eve of the collapse of the Second International', for this collapse is central to an understanding of Lenin's arguments in all his major writings on imperialism. In other words, Lenin's concept of imperialism could only be developed at that level of abstraction which relates to particular social formations and it has a specific place in the particular conjuncture of 1914–18. On the other hand, it does not follow that imperialism is separate from the periodisation of the *mode* into stages nor that it exclusively involves concepts at the level of the social formation. Imperialism is to be understood in the same way as other phenomena, as the complex outcome of more basic forces than are immediately observable.

Lenin's powerful insight in developing the concept can be seen precisely in these terms. Concerned with the conjuncture of the social formation dominated by France, Britain, Germany, Russia and the USA, he did not merely describe that conjuncture, but instead analysed it on the basis of concepts drawn from the periodisations suggested in Chapter 7 and Section 9.1. Lenin identified the characteristics of the stages of monopoly capital and the export of capital, the latter primarily in the form of money capital. It was the articulation of these two highly abstract stages in a world made up of the social formations of Britain, France, etc., with their concrete histories, interrelations and, most importantly, relations with social formations dominated by pre-capitalist modes of production – it was this articulation which Lenin named imperialism.

This immediately raises the question of whether imperialism is a concept appropriate to the present stage of capitalism. Currently state supervision rather than regulation through the credit mechanism is the order of the day and, while the export of capital continues to dominate capitalism's international relations, the most significant form of this internationalisation is productive capital. Thus what we have named state monopoly capitalism and the internationalisation of productive capital (rather than monopoly capitalism and the internationalisation of financial capital) dominate, and the concept of imperialism in the *strict* sense as developed by Lenin is no longer appropriate. The present stage is one where particular aspects of imperialism survive in new forms (for example, the phenomenon described by Lenin as the subjugation of one nation by another) but where other aspects are so transformed that they appear to be qualitatively different. In particular, inter-imperialist rivalry has undergone major transformations and its nature is the subject of dispute. Related to this is the debate over the role of the national state in the present stage of capitalism. These debates are examined in a subsequent section. First, it is necessary to construct a 'composite picture' of the current stage of capitalism in which to locate them.

As we have seen, the current period of capitalism is marked by two tendencies: increasing state intervention in economic reproduction and increasing internationalisation of productive capital. These are stimulated by the intensification of crises and the class struggle associated with them, and by the competitive international expansion of capital. Only by state intervention to promote internationalisation can both tendencies be satisfied and intervention along these lines does predominate. But at times the state's responsibility of guaranteeing social reproduction can be an obstacle to international expansion, whilst conversely the international dimensions of economic crises can further intensify the contradictions of social reproduction. These general observations, however, raise more questions than they answer. In particular, what are their implications for inter-imperialist rivalry and imperialist domination, and the associated role played by national states?

In Lenin's treatment, inter-imperialist rivalry as an economic struggle took the form of the division of the world among competing blocs of capital ('capital associations'). This was linked to political struggle, marked by competitive colonisations and inter-imperialist wars and comprising definite political alliances. The 'capital associations' with which Lenin was concerned were cartels and trusts which, corresponding to the predominance of the internationalisation of commodity and financial capital, divided the world into markets and spheres for lending. Today also 'capital associations' exist, but as multinational corporations competing for the division of the world into markets, financial areas, *and* production bases. This corresponds to the dominance of productive capital as the form which is internationalised. These blocs of capital ('capital associations' in their new form) and today's national states are again the agents in inter-imperialist rivalry. But the form taken by these rivalries in both economic and political struggle has been transformed, first because of the transformations in the nature of the capital associations themselves (from cartels to multinational corporations) and, second because of the increasing role played by state economic intervention. This has resulted in an increasing complexity in inter-imperialist relations and the word 'rivalry' is far from adequate to grasp it. For inter-imperialist rivalry implies also cooperation between blocs of capital and between national states – in Lenin's day in the form of cartels and political and military alliances – and the respective elements around which cooperation and rivalry occur in the present period are transformed. It follows that a general assertion of inter-imperialist rivalry is sterile; analysis requires examination of the particular antagonism and cooperation which arise when the mode of production is at the SMC stage and capital is internationalised as productive capital. Studies of some of the particular aspects of antagonism and rivalry are surveyed in this chapter.

So far we have only discussed state economic intervention in the context of the stage of SMC and divorced from the existence of national states in the world economy. As a result interventions in international economic relations have been absent. As observed earlier, these involve promoting the internationalisation of capital – but subject to the necessity of guaranteeing social reproduction. Accordingly the international economic policies adopted by each national state are subject to the internal forces generated by class struggle and the external forces imposed by international capital and class antagonisms on a world scale. Consequently the policies concerned do not exhibit a simple correspondence with conflicting interests of classes or fractions of classes; a devaluation of sterling, for example, should not be seen as being simply a tactic in the struggle between British proletariat and British bourgeoisie.

Any general discussion of the role played by national states in the current period should not be divorced from the existence of international state apparatuses (such as the IMF and EEC), which are particular products of a world economy in which national states make economic interventions and consequently can form international economic organisations. If we recall that the national state fulfils the fundamental role of guaranteeing social reproduction and that it also acts as an agent of competition, the question is posed whether international state apparatuses are concerned fundamentally with social reproduction, with the resolution of inter-imperialist rivalries or with both. As agents of social reproduction, these bodies can clearly perform the function of organising cooperation to moderate the effects of and implement imperialist domination through the international control of finance, tariffs, etc. In addition the working classes of all national states can be disciplined and moderated in class struggle by the economic control exercised by these bodies, a control that is remote from the struggles at the point of production. It is these functions that we take to be primary in the workings of international bodies, but doing so does not imply that they remain neutral in inter-imperialist rivalries and only represent all capital against all workers. Rather they will be constructed and forced to promote the internationalisation of capital according to the relative strengths of different blocs of capital in competition, just as exchange relations promote a particular centralisation of capital. The difference is that the forces of competition become directly political in character with, for example, the pressure to intensify the effects of economic crisis in particular countries corresponding both to the conditions of working-class struggle (including those expressed through the state apparatuses) and particular inter-ests in inter-imperialist rivalry.

9.3   Imperialist Relations and National States

The transformations in the form of imperialist relations have in recent years stimulated attempts to analyse the role of national states. Several writers, well-represented by Murray (1971), Warren (1971), Rowthorn (1971), consider the problem in terms of a specific question: has the international-isation of capital weakened the capitalist national state as an institution? We shall note below that others such as Poulant-zas (1975) have criticised the question itself as well as the concepts and method employed in answering it. For the moment, however, let us consider the answers which have been provided.

Murray (1971) argues that in general it is the case that the internationalisation of capital has weakened the power of individual national states. He reasons that the capitals of each country are in various ways 'supported' by 'their' national states. The national state performs certain functions in re-spect of its national capital, but this capital has a tendency toward international expansion. For Murray the question then becomes whether the national state performs these required functions for the territorially expanded capital or whether these functions are performed by other state bodies; either foreign states or international bodies such as the EEC. The conclusion is that the national state may continue to exercise the functions required by 'its' national capital, but that the dominant type of internationalisation of capital since World War II has been such that the expanded national capital takes as its supporters national states other than its own, and also international organisations; and this weakens the powers of national states. In effect, Murray sets up a model in which national states compete to perform economic functions for capital, the internationalisation of capital intensifying that competition and consequently strengthening capital at the expense of national states.

Murray's argument has specific weaknesses, some of which are noted by Warren (1971). His list of the necessary functions performed by states for capitals is arbitrarily constructed. It is based upon a false concept of the state intervening from outside into capital's economic processes; it fails to distinguish between the state's role under SMC and that in earlier stages; and it presents the state's economic functions as being for and determined by the needs of capital rather than class struggles, as if the state were a simple tool of the bourgeoisie. His theory of 'competitive nations' leads him to consider international bodies as internationally organised competitors for state economic functions, rather than as institutions complementing and controlling the national state's role as agent of competition and social reproduction.

Murray's concept of the state's economic functions prevents him from periodising capitalism into stages (preventing the use of the concept of SMC), his concept of internationalisation is so ill-defined that he is similarly unable to consider the different historical stages of capital's expansion (the predominance in later stages of the internationalisation of productive capital). However, Murray does take that view that internationalisation as such is, on its present scale, a distinctly modern phenomenon. This permits Warren (1971) to depict the essence of Murray's argument as a simple conclusion derived from mistaken premises: that since the capitalist national state's economic functions have, according to Murray, been performed in one form or another since the beginning of capitalism whereas the internationalisation of capital is a recent phenomenon, the relative significance of these two factors has altered and internationalisation has decreased the national state's role in performing these given functions.

Warren, by contrast, emphasises the increased strength of the national state in relation to capital. He notes the distinctive feature of the state monopoly capitalist stage – the increase in the economic role of the state – and the fact that capital's expansion is dominated by the internationalisation of productive capital. And he notes that national states have themselves instigated this internationalisation, the creation of international state bodies such as the EEC, and the creation of monopolistic firms. Warren's argument however is, like Murray's rather impressionistic and suffers from an inadequate theoretical basis. For one thing, the fact that national states have played a significant role in stimulating internationalisation, the EEC and monopolies is not sufficient to establish that they have control over or dominate capital: the role itself may, in principle, result from the needs of capital and may have the effect of serving to weaken the national state. For another, Warren offers little theoretical reasoning to explain why the power of the national state over capital is increasing. He merely suggests that it results from the growing size of firms (since increased size and decreased numbers make for technically easier control) and the growth of state economic activities. This growth is itself unexplained except in terms of the need to overcome the shocks to which capitalism is subject and in terms of the self-expanding nature of state intervention.

One of the weaknesses of Warren's article (and to a lesser extent of Murray's) is that the power of the national state is considered only in relation to that of that country's capital. The question considered is whether the state institutions are dominated by the international firms into which the country's capital is organised or vice versa. Rowthorn (1971), Mandel (1970), Nicolaus (1970) and others consider the matter from the point of view which Warren neglects: whether the national state, representing a particular national capital, is dominated and weakened by other national states representing their capitals. The view taken by Mandel and Nicolaus, and to some extent by Rowthorn, is that the strength of the national state *vis-à-vis* others depends upon the strength of its national capital. Rowthorn qualifies this view by arguing that in some instances strong capitals can weaken the power of the national state, for a strong capital may be an internationalised capital and 'its' state may therefore pursue the interests of international capital and be subject to another national state which has world hegemony. This qualification fails to overcome the basic problems inherent in the notion that the strength of the national state is related to the strength of the national capital. These problems relate to the fact that the concept of strength or power (of the national state or capital), the concept of national capital, and the concept of the multinational firm are either undefined or else incorrectly specified.

This problem is a serious one not only for those writers such as Rowthorn, Mandel and Nicolaus, who are concerned with the relations between different national capitals (represented by national states), but even more so for Murray and Warren who are concerned with the relations between national states on the one hand and national capitals on the other. It is a product of the attempt to analyse the current period of capitalism with concepts drawn (correctly or otherwise) from an earlier period of less complex determination. Accordingly capitals are associated with particular countries whose states represent them with a degree of strength against other national states and their associated capitals. The absence of a developed concept of strength leads these writers to concentrate on symptoms. As Lenin argued in *Imperialism*: 'In order to understand what is taking place, it is necessary to know what questions are settled by changes in strength. The question as to whether these changes are "purely" economic or *non*-economic (e.g. military) is a secondary one which cannot in the least affect fundamental views on the latest epoch of capitalism. To substitute the question of the form of the struggle and agreements . . . for the question of the *substance* of the struggle and agreements between capital associations is to sink to the role of a sophist'. In general these contributors have merely dealt with the symptoms of international conflict without revealing the substance that underlies them since the two do not correspond in a simple fashion to some concept of national states' economic or political strength. Moreover, the concept of power employed by these authors is that which is appropriate to a zero-sum game (each capital or nation loses what the other gains) and this, as Poulantzas (1973) argues, is not the Marxist concept of power.

Poulantzas (1975) advances the debate over the relation-ship between the national state and capital by radically ex-amining the concepts employed in the discussion so far consi-dered. Poulantzas characterises the state as having no power of its own, but instead expressing and crystallising class powers. This provides an immediate critique of those who pose the question of the relative power of the state and capital; for Poulantzas the relevant question is the relative powers of the classes and fractions expressed in and through the state. In the context of internationalisation these groups include internal and international fractions of the bourgeoisie. Moreover, understanding that the state expres-ses the crystallisation of class powers saves Poulantzas from adopting the view implicit to a greater or lesser extent in Murray and Rowthorn that the position of the national state relates to the economic power and requirements of capital; for on the one hand it is not only economic but also political and ideological class relations which determine the state's functions, and on the other it is not only the classes represen-tative of capital, the bourgeoisies, which determine the na-tional state but the relations between all classes and fractions.

Thus, Poulantzas's (1975) concept of the state is complete-ly destructive of the work surveyed so far in this section. But what alternative analysis of the national state does he adopt? He argues that the relevant effects of internationalisation for the national state occur through its effects on the class struc-ture – and particularly the structure of the fractions of the bourgeoisie – within the country. Thus for him the problem of the relationship between multinationals such as ICI and the British state is to be analysed in terms of the relative strengths in class relations of, among others, the international and internal fractions of the bourgeoisie and the fractions of the proletariat. Similarly the interests of American or other capitals affect the British state, according to Poulantzas, to the extent that they affect the class structure of Britain.

As a critique of the state power versus the power of multinationals' question Poulantzas's argument is convinc-ing. However, its positive contribution to a theory of the current period suffers from its dependence upon an inade-quate understanding of the current stage of capitalism. In keeping with his treatment of the relative autonomy of political relations, he underestimates the role played by the state in economic reproduction (in response to class struggle), subordinating this to a chain of imperialism headed by the USA in which the internationalisation of production sweeps all before it. Paradoxically, this is coupled with an over-estimation of the role of the national state in social reproduction at the expense of the role played by international state apparatuses. In fact these are treated as if their significance is small. He argues that the national state's economic functions are inseparable from its ideological and political functions and therefore cannot be effectively transferred or taken over but only, in a limited way, delegated to the international institutions. The argument is used to support the conclusion that political strategies which 'defend' the national state against these apparatuses are necessarily reformist, a conclusion that is clearly present in the premise that abstracts from the significance of state economic intervention.

If we give explicit consideration to these international apparatuses and apply to them the principles Poulantzas applied to the national state the opposite political assessment would result. Taking them seriously as state apparatuses the power they exert is not their own but is a crystallisation of class powers. It is then possible to discuss the nature of the class relations which are expressed in these institutions. A paper by the Balance of Payments Study Group (1977) takes this approach and argues that the international apparatuses such as the EEC and IMF express in an extremely onesided manner the political interests of the bourgeoisies or, to be more precise, those bourgeois fractions which represent internationalised capital. In this they differ from national states since the latter, acting as the factor of cohesion for social formations, pursue policies directly determined by the relative powers and strengths of the bourgeois and proletarian classes and fractions. The ability of the capitalist national state to act on behalf of capital is affected by the possibility of class conflict (at the minimum, electoral defeat for bourgeois representatives) to an extent which is not the case for international state apparatuses. Moreover the international institutions themselves occupy unequal positions in this respect, with some such as the IMF being more loosely connected with antagonistic class relations than others (such as the EEC).

From this perspective it is clearly wrong of Poulantzas to pose the problem as one of whether or not the national state transfers its role to international state apparatuses. Instead there exists a complex structure of national and international capitalist state apparatuses, some of which are more distanced from the site of class struggles (the national social formation) than others. Those which are more distanced are more freely able to pursue the class interests and class positions of the dominant bourgeois fractions than is the national state. Because they have mechanisms (laws, treaties, agreements) for enforcing policies onto their constituent national states this structure of international institutions is able to exert what appears as an outside pressure on national states in favour of the interests of internationalised capital. For this reason a political strategy which attacks the international institutions is by no means reformist; it is an attack on the whole structure of capitalist state apparatuses, and it weakens the constraints which in various ways hinder an attack on the national state itself.

9.4   International Unity and Rivalry

As every child knows, Lenin correctly identified rivalry as the distinguishing feature of imperialism. Blocs of capital were easily identified with particular national states; and economic antagonism between these blocs, giving rise directly to political antagonism between their respective states, predominated and overwhelmed the elements of cooperation. Many Marxist writers, considering inter-imperialist relations today, simply adopt the identical thesis (see for example Bullock and Yaffe (1975)). This gives them an appearance of being faithful to Leninist principles but it is a spurious appearance. In fact they abandon Leninist principles by forgetting that for Lenin imperialism is a particular stage (the articulation of monopoly capitalism and the internationalisation of finance capital). In moving from that stage to the present one (SMC and internationalisation of productive capital) inter-imperialist relations have been transformed, and the problem of the relationship between antagonism and cooperation, unity and rivalry, has to be re-examined. Those who fail to recognise these transformations also tend to adopt a simple understanding of international economic relations, either continuing to rely upon a direct correspondence between national capitals and the national state or mistaking the complexity of international rivalry for its disappearance. Such is the breeding ground of unfruitful debates, even though they have concerned the assessment of concrete historical trends. On the one hand writers such as Mandel (1969) (1970) and Szymanski (1977) argue that we are witnessing a decline in the hegemony of United States capital and its political agencies over those of other imperialist centres. Capitals in Western Europe and Japan have developed their relative strength and this development has involved major challenges to American capital, so that the latter cannot be considered the undisputed leader of the block of imperialist capitals. By contrast Nicolaus (1970) and Petras and Rhodes (1976) (1977) argue that United States hegemony has either not been seriously challenged by the other imperialist centres, or that United States capital has regained its hegemony after having suffered serious setbacks. Although this debate is of an empirical nature it has within it important theoretical elements, for underlying it is the question of whether competition or cooperation, unity or rivalry, predominates in inter-imperialist relations.

Mandel (1969) (1970) emphasises the significance of competition for capitalist development and, as an aspect of this, asserts that inter-imperialist relations are necessarily competitive. This is so because of the law of uneven and combined development. Since capitalism develops unevenly, there are always some capitals developing faster than others and these can only do so by competing against the previously dominant capitals (and among themselves) for market shares and areas of operation. The modern appearance of this theoretical proposition, according to Mandel, is the rapid development of West European and Japanese capital based upon their ability to exploit a labour force cheaper than the American working class. These challenge American hegemony but, nevertheless, do not precipitate inter-imperialist war because of the threat from the socialist states. For Mandel, competition and rivalry predominate over cooperation. It is significant that in his work, state economic intervention is analysed predominantly in terms of credit expansion to maintain domestic capital accumulation. It is argued that the national state's expansion of credit is eventually limited by the forces of international competition acting on the resultant inflation, and giving rise to credit cycles. Such an analysis owes more to the bourgeois Keynesian theory of targets and instruments than it does to the Marxist theory of accumulation.

For Nicolaus (1970), on the other hand, internationalisation has proceeded to a point where the interdependence of capitals renders meaningless any theory of competition between nationally or regionally organised blocs of capital. Nicolaus emphasises that world capitalism must be seen as a whole; rather than separate national or regional capitals in conflict with each other there is one complex system whose centre is located in United States social relations. The proponents of each of these positions argue that the other has abandoned the classical Marxist position. Mandel (1970) argues that Nicolaus has adopted the concept of ultra-imperialism put forward by Kautsky and attacked by Lenin, although he also reports (1975) that Nicolaus has characterised as Kautskyist Mandel's own concept of the formation of a West European imperialist bloc out of the several imperialist powers. In passing it should be observed that Mandel's theorisation of the need for a European state to correspond to a European capital consists of a crude determination of political from economic relations (for a discussion of which see Holloway (1976)).

In the debate, those who simply emphasise inter-imperialist rivalry have often developed indices of imperial strength. The problems with these are indicative of the inadequacy of analysing complex categories with simple ones. Mandel (1969) (1970), for example, measures the strenth of a nation's capital partly by the nation's export performance and, in addition, considers the ability of a region's (or nation's) capital to compete as dependent partly on wage costs in that region. Therefore he is necessarily thinking of a nation's capital as being that capital which is actually operated within that national state, irrespective of ownership. For this he is taken to task by Nicolaus (1970), who points out that ownership complicates matters, that profits controlled by the American bourgeoisie emanate in part from subsidiaries operating in other national states and that, therefore, the capital operating in those countries cannot be identified as being 'their' capital in competition with American capital. Elsewhere Mandel argues that whether a particular national state is strong enough to lead the imperialist bloc depends on whether its capital is the owner of capitals located abroad to a sufficient extent; ownership of assets abroad becomes the dominant index. Even if one accepts the concept of national blocs of capital implied in this approach, these indices are inadequate measures of a capital's strength. If 'strength' refers to the national capital's ability to accumulate at a rapid rate, the appropriate criterion of a capital's strength is its profitability. Export performance is only relevant to this in the very indirect sense of being partially related to the productivity of labour in the nation. The profitability of a national bloc of capital depends partially on this productivity but the connection is so loose that to take exports as an index is quite futile. The exports and productivity in Britain of a firm which can be identified as British capital may be low, yet its profitability may be extremely high as a result of its overseas operations. The ownership of capital abroad is relevant to profitability only to the extent that its ownership reflects or influences the profitability of the parent capital. In any case, as Poulantzas (1975) argues in a polemic against Mandel, the significance of the ownership of foreign assets cannot be estimated in terms of a simple quantitative measure. Poulantzas argues that ownership of capital located abroad (or, in flow terms, the export of capital) is indeed the most significant index of strength in and domination by a particular national capital, but the characteristics of this export of capital are as important as its size; the question of whether it is direct or portfolio investment, of which sectors it goes into, and of the degree of concentration of the industries into which the capital flows. Another approach to the index question is that of the Cambridge Political Economy Group (1974). Representing a view which is common in Britain, not unnaturally in view of Britain's balance-of-payments history, the authors tend to treat the nation's balance of payments as an indicator of its capital's strength in inter-imperialist conflicts. This suffers from the same fault as does the use of exports as an index, but it is even less connected with the productivity and profitability of locally operated capital than is export performance. Significantly all these indices, whatever their economic merits, remain aloof from the role of political power and working-class struggle.

9.5   Uneven Development

In the preceding section we have examined the problem of the relations between advanced capitalist national states. The capitalist system, however, embraces countries at different stages of development. The so-called Third World exists at the opposite pole from advanced capitalist nations, and the theory of imperialist relations is incomplete unless it can grasp the dominance of the advanced sector over the backward sector. Indeed for many this dominance is precisely what is meant by imperialism.

The problems involved in analysing these relations are best seen in relation to the work of Frank (1969) (1972). He presents a radical thesis with the following components. All countries which participate in the capitalist world market are capitalist; their economic relations are those of the capitalist mode of production. Nevertheless, through their participation in the market, the less advanced are exploited as countries by the advanced capitalist nations. The latter are the metropolises, the former the periphery (although there are sub-metropolises between the two) and their interrelation is such that the increasing wealth of the metropolis has its necessary counterpart in the decreasing wealth of the periphery ('the development of underdevelopment'). This process, he argues, has been occurring in essentially unchanged form since the beginnings of capitalism in the advanced nations. Frank's thesis is radical in the sense that it provides a basis for a moral polemic against the advanced capitalist nations. It is also to be associated with the political strategies of nationalism (rather than class struggle). It is not, however, a Marxist thesis. From a Marxist perspective, each of its elements has to be rejected as we shall show.

Laclau (1971), in a classic critique of Frank, demonstrates the invalidity of his first thesis in particular. The fact that the economy of a peasant village in Latin America is either directly or indirectly affected by capital's international expansion and creation of the world market does not mean that the economic (and social) relations under which the peasants are exploited are those of the capitalist mode of production. The mode of production may be non-capitalist, even if production is ultimately for the capitalist world market. The minimum condition for the mode of production to be capitalist is that labour is exploited through labour-power itself being a commodity, but this is by no means a necessary concomitant of production for the world market. The issue which is involved here is paralleled by the issue at stake in the productive/unproductive labour dispute. The question is whether social formations (sectors) which do not have specifically capitalist relations of production are nevertheless capitalist (produce surplus value) because the use values they produce are exchanged on the capitalist world market (with capital). In the productive/unproductive labour dispute the question is particularly acute when it comes to considering the relationship between domestic labour and the capitalist mode of production; whether domestic labour constitutes a separate mode of production and whether it produces values (see Fine and Harris (1976)).

In addition Frank's notion that the dominated countries are capitalist, with capitalist relations of production, fails to distinguish between a mode of production and a social formation. The dominated countries are social formations. As such they are the product of an articulation of different modes of production. Therefore even if capitalist relations of production were dominant within this articulation (and as a rule they are not) it would be wrong to characterise these formations as the effect of the capitalist mode of production pure and simple.

The second element of Frank's thesis, that the dominated countries are exploited by the advanced through their market participation, is inconsistent with Marx's concept of exploitation. The most basic point is that exploitation is a relation between classes and not between nations. Related to this is the fact that capitalist exploitation cannot take place through exchange; surplus value can only be created through capitalist control of production rather than exchange. Frank is, therefore, totally at odds with the Marxist approach in treating exploitation at the level of market exchange between nations. In this he is accompanied by Emmanuel (1972) (who is also criticised by Bettelheim in an appendix). Emmanuel argues that one country is exploited by another and that this occurs through unequal exchange. The argument is developed in a neo-Ricardian manner, theorising unequal exchange in terms of the exchange values which result from unequal value compositions of capital. Unequal exchange, therefore, is simply the idea that since the ratios of exchange values are not the same as those of living labour embodied, the countries with the higher value compositions of capital appropriate through exchange more labour than has been expended in their own lines of production. In addition it is complemented by the argument that, while rates of profit are equalised worldwide through the international mobility of money-capital, real wage rates are not equalised and this is the source of further exploitation of one country by another.

The third element in Frank's theory is that underdevelopment is produced and increasingly reproduced by the development of the advanced capitalist nations. This development destroys the pre-capitalist industries in the Third World, draws those nations into the capitalist market and, by appropriating surplus from them, prevents them from accumulating capital. The thesis is clearly invalid for Marxists as long as Frank fails to specify how surplus is appropriated in some way other than unequal exchange. But even a Marxist formulation of the thesis that surplus is appropriated by capitals in the advanced capitalist countries is not sufficient to demonstrate that the backwardness of the rest of the world is thereby increased. The appropriation of surplus is the basis of capital's expanded reproduction, so that an increase in capitalist development in the Third World does occur in consequence of this appropriation. Warren (1973) in fact attempts to show on empirical grounds that the international expansion of capital has been responsible for a remarkable development in the manufacturing sector of the Third World economies (criticisms of which are voiced by McMichael, Petras and Rhodes (1974)).

Lastly, Frank's thesis that the advanced capitalist nations have appropriated surplus in essentially the same way since the beginning of capitalism denies the specificity of the concept of imperialism. This contrasts strongly with the Marxist concept, developed by Lenin, that imperialism is a specific stage of capitalism. To say this is not to deny that capital has from its beginning had a tendency to create the world market, but unlike Frank it is to emphasise the fact that capital expands internationally *as capital* and that this export of capital takes a succession of differing forms.

These are the criticisms of Frank's thesis and related work in outline. We return now to the question of unequal exchange and consider it in more detail for it is a pervasive thesis in both its forms; in the idea that unequal value compositions of capital lead to unequal exchange, and that low real wages in the Third World do so. The thesis is based on the idea that labour in both the Third World and the advanced capitalist nations produces values. It is clearly situated, therefore, within Frank's thesis that the whole world can be thought of as the direct manifestation of the capitalist mode of production since values are not produced in pre-capitalist modes. This mode of production can be divided into nations, but then their basis is only antagonism between capitals (which is itself based on the fundamental antagonism, class struggle between proletariat and bourgeoisie). The effect of this is that the laws of development at an economic level cannot be properly studied and, in addition, political struggle is misunderstood. The economic laws of development which can be postulated at this level are those such as concentration and centralisation, and general crises: laws of the mode of production. It is impossible to analyse the transformation of pre-capitalist relations of production which is forced by the articulation between pre-capitalist and capitalist modes. Similarly at the political level it is impossible to analyse such phenomena as peasant uprisings. And the effects on national states of antagonisms between classes and class fractions which are not within the explicitly capitalist framework of bourgeoisie-proletariat (the role or even existence of *comprador* and pre-capitalist land-owning classes) cannot be considered.

The economic laws and the political analysis of imperialist relations between advanced capitalist and other modes of production can only be achieved by abandoning this method. This requires two things. First, a recognition that other modes of production are precisely other modes and rejection of the thesis that the whole world is capitalist. This immediately implies that imperialist relations pertain to social formations (which result from particular articulations of modes of production) and that is the proper level for their analysis. Second, an explicit recognition that imperialist relations are of a political as well as an economic structure and that politics has an effect on economic reproduction. There are several examples of the phenomena which may be rigorously examined using this approach of Frank and Emmanuel. The question of why less-advanced techniques and lower wages exist in the backward nations is something which, as we have seen, cannot be answered in the framework of unequal exchange even though their existence is the basis for the theory. For the theory tells us that unequal exchange gives rise to exploitation and the development of underdevelopment without being able to tell us why the surplus is not then accumulated in 'foreign investment' in the backward countries. It can, however, be answered in terms of the political effect of the articulation of different modes of production. For this articulation gives rise to political alliances of various types. In one such, the interests of foreign bourgeoisies dominate and these interests are themselves contradictory. On the one hand they seek to expand capital as capital in the backward country. On the other, capital cannot be created overnight, pre-capitalist relations cannot be abolished by decree, so the expansion of capitalist relations develops side by side with the maintenance of pre-capitalist relations. This co-existence is contradictory. It affects the capitalist relations themselves, but it also ensures that the pre-capitalist relations are affected. Their co-existence with capitalist relations does in many cases lead to an intensification of the extraction of surplus labour and therefore an apparent strengthening of pre-capitalist relations. How this comes about is easily seen. The pre-capitalist enterprises are forced to compete with the capitalist as long as they survive and in so far as they produce commodities, and the only way that they can do so while still yielding surplus labour to the exploiting class is by an intensification of the existing mode of exploitation. This can lead to a strengthening of the pre-capitalist elements in the ruling bloc and therefore the maintenance for a considerable time of the political conditions of existence of the pre-capitalist economy. From this point of view, therefore, it is possible to see why less advanced techniques are used: they are associated with the maintenance of non-capitalist modes of production rather than with the spread of the capitalist mode to embrace every field and workshop. Similar analysis of the political alliances generated by the articulation of the modes of production would permit us to see how the interests of foreign bourgeoisies, represented in these alliances, forces the depression of the value of wages in the backward country below that of the advanced national states and how this is associated with the establishment of capitalist production alongside pre-capitalist.

The emphasis that we place on the political element and the influence of politics on economics in this analysis serves as a sharp reminder that imperialist relations can never be fully grasped if considered as economic in abstraction from politics. This is especially so in the case of relations between advanced capitalist social formations and social formations dominated by pre-capitalist modes. In the latter case, the transformation of the pre-capitalist into capitalist social formations with all its contradictions, including the temporary intensification of pre-capitalist modes of production, cannot be carried out solely by the forces of competition in the world market and the internal contradictions of the existing relations and forces or production. No equivalent of 'primitive accumulation' of capital can take place internally without political intervention since the capitals formed thereby would be unable to compete on the world market with advanced capitals. And capital cannot be expanded by the import of capital from the advanced capitalist countries as an 'automatic' economic process. Since political power necessarily involves control of national boundaries and international transactions, it is only if the ruling classes (power bloc) permit its entry that foreign capital can become established. Hence the exact structure of the power bloc becomes crucial in determining the extent to which the economic relations of the capitalist mode are established and come into conflict with those of the pre-capitalist modes.

For this reason politics plays a major role. There is pressure for the interests of foreign bourgeoisies to have a place within the power bloc of backward national states. There is also pressure for fundamental changes in the power bloc in the other direction; toward a nationalist, anti-imperialist, and in some cases socialist regime. But to say this is to point to the fact that even here, where politics is so significant, economic relations are determinant. For the pressure for the representation of foreign bourgeoisies in the political alliance is the outcome of capital's need for expansion. And the opposite pressure, for an anti-imperialist or a socialist alliance, stems ultimately from the class struggles produced by capital's expansion, and the disruption of existing modes of production which ensues.

Bibliography

(*CSEB*=Bulletin of the Conference of Socialist Economists)

Althusser, L. (1969), *For Marx* (London: Allen Lane, The Penguin Press).
Althusser, L., and Balibar, E. (1970), *Reading 'Capital'* (London: New Left Books).
Arthur, C. J. (1976), 'The Concept of Abstract Labour', *CSEB*, vol. v.2.14 (October).
Balance of Payments Study Group (CPGB) (1977), 'The Balance of Payments', *Economic Bulletin* (Autumn).
Baran, P., and Sweezy, P. (1964), *Monopoly Capital* (New York: Monthly Review Press).
Barker, C. (1978), 'A Note on the Theory of Capitalist States', *Capital and Class*, 4 (Spring).
Baumol, W. J. (1974), 'The Transformation Problem: What Marx Really Meant', *Journal of Economic Literature* (March).
Bhaduri, A. (1969), 'On the Significance of Recent Controversies in Capital Theory: A Marxian View', *Economic Journal*, vol. 79.
Bleaney, M. (1976), *Underconsumption Theories* (London: Lawrence & Wishart).
Braverman, H. (1974), *Labor and Monopoly Capital* (New York: Monthly Review Press).
Brighton Labour Process Group (1977), 'The Capitalist Labour Process', *Capital and Class*, 1 (Spring).
Brunhoff, S. de (1976), *Marx on Money* (New York: Urizen Books).
Bullock, P. (1973), 'Categories of Labour Power for Capital', *CSEB*, vol. II.6 (Autumn).
Bullock, P. (1974), 'Defining Productive Labour for Capital', *CSEB*, vol. III.9 (Autumn).
Bullock, P., and Yaffe, D. (1975), 'Inflation, Crisis and the Post-War Boom', *Revolutionary Communist*, 3/4 (November).
Cambridge Political Economy Group (1974), *Britain's Economic Crisis* (Spokesman Pamphlet, no. 44).
Catephores, G. (1973), 'Some Remarks on the Falling Rate of Profit', *CSEB*, vol. II.5 (Spring).

Catephores, G., and Morishima, M. (1978), *Exploitation, Population, and Growth* (Maidenhead: McGraw-Hill).

Clarke, S. (1977), 'Marxism, Sociology and Poulantzas' Theory of the State', *Capital and Class*, 2 (Summer).

Cogoy, M. (1973), 'The Fall of the Rate of Profit and the Theory of Accumulation: A Reply to Paul Sweezy', *CSEB*, vol. II.7 (Winter).

Cutler, A., Hindess, B, Hirst, P., and Hussain, A. (1977) and (1978), *Marx's Capital and Capitalism Today*, vols. 1 and 2 (London: Routledge & Kegan Paul).

Dawson, W. H. (1891), *Bismarck and State Socialism* (London: Sonnenschein).

Emmanuel, A. (1972), *Unequal Exchange* (London: New Left Books).

Ergas, H., and Fishman, D. (1975), 'The Marxian Theory of Money and the Crisis of Capital', *CSEB*, vol. IV.11 (June).

Fine, B. (1973), 'A Note on Productive and Unproductive Labour', *CSEB*, vol. II.6 (Autumn).

Fine, B. (1975a), 'The Circulation of Capital, Ideology and Crisis', *CSEB*, vol. IV.12 (October).

Fine, B. (1975b), 'From Marx to Morishima', *CSEB*, vol. IV.12 (October).

Fine, B. (1975c), *Marx's 'Capital'* (London: Macmillan).

Fine, B., and Harris, L. (1975), 'The British Economy since March 1974', *CSEB*, vol. IV.12 (October).

Fine, B., and Harris, L. (1976a), 'State Expenditure in Advanced Capitalism: A Critique', *New Left Review*, no. 98 (July/August).

Fine, B., and Harris, L. (1976b), 'The British Economy: May 1975–January 1976', *CSEB*, vol. V.14 (June).

Fine, B., and Harris, L. (1976c), 'Controversial Issues in Marxist Economic Theory', in R. Miliband and J. Saville, *Socialist Register 1976* (London: Merlin Press).

Fine, B., and Harris, L. (1977), 'Surveying the Foundations', *Socialist Register 1977*, ed. R. Miliband and J. Saville (London: Merlin Press).

Frank, A. G. (1969), *Capitalism and Underdevelopment in Latin America* (New York: Monthly Review Press).

Frank, A. G. (1972), *Lumpenbourgeoisie: Lumpendevelopment* (New York: Monthly Review Press).

Fraser, D., ed. (1976), *The New Poor Law in the Nineteenth Century* (London: Macmillan).

Gamble, A., and Walton, P. (1976), *Capitalism in Crisis* (London: Macmillan).

Gerstein, I. (1976), 'Production, Circulation, and Value: The Significance of the "Transformation Problem" in Marx's Critique of Political Economy', *Economy and Society*, V.3 (August).

Gillman, J. M. (1957), *The Falling Rate of Profit* (London: Dobson).

Glyn, A. (1972), 'Capitalist Crisis and the Organic Composition', *CSEB*, vol. I.2 (Winter).

Glyn, A. (1973), 'Productivity, Organic Composition and the Falling Rate of Profit – A Reply', *CSEB*, vol. II.6 (Autumn).

Glyn, A., and Sutcliffe, R. (1972), *British Capitalism, Workers and the Profit Squeeze* (Harmondsworth: Penguin Books).

Gordon, D. (1975), 'Capital *v.* Labor: The Current Crisis in the Sphere of Production', in *Radical Perspectives on the Economic Crisis of Monopoly Capitalism* (New York: Union for Radical Political Economics).

Gough, I. (1972), 'Marx's Theory of Productive and Unproductive Labour', *New Left Review*, 76.

Gough, I. (1973), 'On Productive and Unproductive Labour – A Reply', *CSEB*, vol. II.7 (Winter).

Gough, I. (1975), 'State Expenditure in Capitalism', *New Left Review 92*.

Gough, I., and Harrison, J. (1975), 'Unproductive Labour and Housework Again', *CSEB*, vol. IV.10 (February).

Harris, L. (1976), 'On Interest, Credit and Capital', *Economy and Society*, vol. 5.2 (May).

Harris, L. (1978), 'The Science of the Economy', *Economy and Society*, vol. 7.3 (August).

Harrison, J. (1973*a*), 'Productive and Unproductive Labour in Marx's Political Economy', *CSEB*, vol. II.6 (Autumn).

Harrison, J. (1973*b*), 'The Political Economy of Housework', *CSEB*, vol. II.7 (Winter).

Harvey, J. (1977), 'Theories of Inflation', *Marxism Today*, vol. XXI.1 (January).

Himmelweit, S. (1974), 'The Continuing Saga of the Falling Rate of Profit – A Reply to Mario Cogoy', *CSEB*, vol. III.9 (Autumn).

Hindess, B., and Hirst, P. (1977), *Mode of Production and Social Formation* (London: Macmillan).

Hodgson, G. (1974), 'The Theory of the Falling Rate of Profit', *New Left Review*, 84.

Hodgson, G. (1976), 'Exploitation and Embodied Labour Time', *CSEB*, vol. V.13 (February).

Hodgson, G. (1977), 'Papering Over the Cracks', *Socialist Register 1977*, ed. R. Miliband and J. Saville (London: Merlin Press).

Hodgson, G., and Steedman, I. (1975), 'Fixed Capital and Value Analysis', *CSEB*, vol. V.1 (June).

Holloway, J. (1976), 'Some Issues Raised by Marxist Analyses of European Integration', *CSEB*, vol. V.1 (March).

Holloway, J., and Picciotto, S. (1976), 'A Note on the Theory of the State', *CSEB*, vol. V.14 (June).

Holloway, J., and Picciotto, S. (1977), 'Capital, Crisis and the State', *Capital and Class*, 2 (Summer).

Howell, P. (1975), 'Once Again on Productive and Unproductive Labour', *Revolutionary Communist*, vol. III/IV (November).

Hussain, A. (1976), 'Hilferding's Finance Capital', *CSEB*, vol. V.1 (March).

Itoh, M. (1975), 'The Formation of Marx's Theory of Crisis', *CSEB*, vol. IV.10 (February).

Kalecki, M. (1943), 'Political Aspects of Full Employment', *Political Quarterly*, vol. XIV.

Kay, G. (1976), 'A Note on Abstract Labour', *CSEB*, vol. V.13 (February).

Keynes, J. M. (1936), *The General Theory of Employment, Interest and Money* (London: Macmillan).

Laclau, E. (1971), 'Feudalism and Capitalism in Latin America', *New Left Review*, 67.

Luxemburg, R. (1963), *The Accumulation of Capital* (London: Routledge & Kegan Paul).

McMichael, P., Petras, J., and Rhodes, R. (1974), 'Imperialism and the Contradictions of Development', *New Left Review*, 85 (May/June).

Mandel, E. (1967), 'International Capitalism and "Supranationality"', in R. Miliband and J. Saville (eds), *Socialist Register 1967* (London: Merlin Press).

Mandel, E. (1969), 'Where is America Going?', *New Left Review*, 54 (March/April).

Mandel, E. (1975), *Late Capitalism* (London: New Left Books).

Mandel, E. (1970), 'The Laws of Unequal Development', *New Left Review*, no. 59 (January/February).

Marglin, S. (1974), 'What do Bosses Do?', *Review of Radical Political Economy* (Summer).

Marx, K. (1968), 'Preface to *A Contribution to the Critique of Political Economy*', in K. Marx and F. Engels, *Selected Works* (London: Lawrence & Wishart).

Marx, K. (1970), *Capital*, vol. I (London: Lawrence & Wishart).

Marx, K. (1972), *Capital*, vol. II (London: Lawrence & Wishart).

Marx, K. (1972), *Capital*, vol. III (London: Lawrence & Wishart).

Marx, K. (1973), *Grundrisse* (Harmondsworth: Penguin Books).

Marx, K. (1976), *Capital*, vol. I (Harmondsworth: Penguin Books).

Meek, R. (1967), *Economics and Ideology, and Other Essays* (London: Chapman & Hall).

Morishima, M. (1973), *Marx's Economics: A Dual Theory of Value and Growth* (Cambridge University Press).

Morishima, M. (1974), 'Marx in the Light of Modern Economic Theory', *Econometrica*.

Morishima, M. (1976), 'Positive Profits with Negative Surplus Value – A Comment', *Economic Journal*, vol. 86 (September).

Murray, R. (1971), 'The Internationalization of Capital and the Nation State', *New Left Review*, 67 (May/June).

Murray, R. (1973), 'Productivity, Organic Composition, and the Falling Rate of Profit', *CSEB*, vol. II.5 (Spring).

Nicolaus, M. (1970), 'The Universal Contradiction', *New Left Review*, no. 59 (January/February).

O'Connor, J. (1973), *The Fiscal Crisis of the State* (New York: St. Martin's Press).

Petras, J. and Rhodes, R. (1976), 'The Reconsolidation U.S. Hegemony', *New Left Review*, 97.

Petras, J. and Rhodes, R. (1977), 'Reply to Critics', *New Left Review*, nos 101/102 (February/April).

Pilling, G. (1972), 'The Law of Value in Ricardo and Marx', *Economy and Society*, vol. I. 3 (August).

Poulantzas, N. (1973), *Political Power and Social Class* (London: New Left Books).

Poulantzas, N. (1975), *Classes in Contemporary Capitalism* (London: New Left Books).

Rosdolsky, R. (1977), *The Making of Marx's 'Capital'* (London: Pluto Press).

Rowthorn, B. (1971), 'Imperialism in the Seventies – Unity or Rivalry?', *New Left Review*, 69 (September/October).

Rowthorn, B. (1973), 'Vulgar Economy', *CSEB*, vol. II.5 (Spring). Reprinted in *New Left Review*, 86 (1974).

Rowthorn, B. (1976), 'Late Capitalism: A Review Article', *New Left Review*, 98.

Samuelson, P. A. (1971), 'Understanding the Marxian Notion of Exploitation: A Summary of the so-called Transformation Problem Between Marxian Values and Competitive Prices', *Journal of Economic Literature*, IX.2.

Seton, F. (1957), 'The "Transformation Problem"', *Review of Economic Studies*, no. 24.

Sraffa, P. (1960), *The Production of Commodities by Means of Commodities* (Cambridge University Press).

Steedman, I. (1972), 'Marx on the Rate of Profit', *CSEB*, vol. I.4 (Winter).

Steedman, I. (1975), 'Positive Profit and Negative Surplus Value', *Economic Journal*, vol. 85 (March).

Steedman, I. (1976), 'Positive Profits with Negative Surplus Value: A Reply', *Economic Journal*, vol. 86 (September), and 'A Reply to Wolfstetter', ibid. (December).

Steedman, I. (1977), *Marx after Sraffa* (London: New Left Books).

Sweezy, P. (1949), *The Theory of Capitalist Development* (New York: Monthly Review Press).

Szymanski, A. (1977), 'Is U.S. Imperialism Resurgent? – A Critique of Petras and Rhodes', *New Left Review*, 101/102 (February/April).

Thompson, G. (1977), 'The Relationship Between the Financial and Industrial Sector in the United Kindom Economy', *Economy and Society*, vol. 6.3 (August).

Tomlinson, E. (1978), 'Althusser, Balibar and Production', *Capital and Class*, 4 (Spring).

Warren, B. (1971), 'The Internationalization of Capital and the Nation State: A Comment', *New Left Review*, 68 (July/August).

Warren, B. (1973), 'Imperialism and Capitalist Development', *New Left Review*, 81 (September/October).

Williams, K. (1975), 'Facing Reality – a Critique of Karl Popper's Empiricism', *Economy and Society*, vol. IV.3 (August).

Wolfstetter, E. (1976), 'Positive Profits with Negative Surplus Value: A Comment', *Economic Journal*, vol. 86 (December).

Yaffe, D. (1972), 'The Marxian Theory of Crisis, Capital and the State',

CSEB, vol. I.4 (Winter). Reprinted in *Economy and Society*, vol. II.2 (1973).

Yaffe, D. (1973), 'The Crisis of Profitability: A Critique of the Glyn–Sutcliffe Thesis', *New Left Review*, 80 (July/August).

Yaffe, D. (1975), 'Value and Price in Marx's *Capital*', *Revolutionary Communist*, vol. I (January).

Index

Figures in **bold type** indicate principal references.

For subdivisions of chapters, *see* CONTENTS, pp. v–vi. These subdivisions are also indexed individually.

'p' means *passim* (here and there), scattered references.

Alphabetical order: Word-by-word.

182   *Index*